TEACHING
YOUR COMPUTER
TO TALK-
a manual of command and response

No. 1330
$15.95

TEACHING YOUR COMPUTER TO TALK—
a manual of command and response

By Edward R. Teja

TAB BOOKS Inc.
BLUE RIDGE SUMMIT, PA. 17214

FIRST EDITION

FIRST PRINTING

Copyright © 1981 by TAB BOOKS Inc.

Printed in the United States of America

Library of Congress Cataloging in Publication Data

Teja, Edward R.
     Teaching your computer to talk—a manual of command and response.

     Includes index.
     1. Speech processing systems.   2. Computer input-output equipment.   I. Title.
TK7882.S65T44   621.3819′532   81-9197
ISBN 0-8306-0019-1   AACR2
ISBN 0-8306-1330-7 (pbk.)

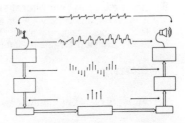

Contents

Preface   **7**

1 Speech Recognition and Synthesis—Why Bother?   **13**
But If It Could Talk—Talking Databases—Dedicated Suppliers—
Helping the Handicapped—Talk to Machines—Learning to Speak
Speech

2 The Speech Process   **34**
The Sounds of Speech—Understanding What Was Meant—The
Physics of Speech—Where You Say It—Speech Parameters—
Putting Sounds Together—A Model Speaker

3 Synthesizing Speech   **44**
From Voders to Prerecorded Voices—The Speech Chips—
Speaking Differently—Speech Without Restriction—Synthesizers
by Themselves

4 Converting Text to Speech   **69**
Match the Synthesizer to the Application—Store Sounds, Not
Words—Programming Produces Phonemes—Parsing a
Word—Establishing the Rules—Mix the Strategies—Uncovering
Word Structures—Speeding Up Things—Buying a System Off the
Shelf—Unrestricted Speech from LPC Chips

5 First, Speech Recognition   **88**
Recognition Isn't Understanding—Drawing Crazy Patterns—The
Recognizers You Can Buy—Low-Cost Recognition—Specialized
Systems—Taking Words Out of Isolation—Listening to
Anyone—Picking a Recognizer

6 Second, Adding a Voice to Your Microcomputer   **114**
From Telecommunications to You—Delta Modulation—The
Simple Approach—Putting a Synthesizer to Work—Other Chatty
Chips—Being Discrete

7 Some Systems Ahead of Their Time   **151**
Ask the Computer About the Weather—A Voice-Controlled
Dialer—Chatty Robots—Flying Safely—And the Beat Goes On

8 Adding Ears to Your Microcomputer   **168**
The Speech Laboratory—A Simple Recognition Peripheral—The
Input Circuit—Making Things Digital—Controlling the World—
Making Sense of Numbers—Improving Recogniton

Glossary   **195**

Appendix A   Equipment Manufacturers   **198**

Appendix B   Additional Reading Material   **204**

Appendix C   ARPABET Symbols   **205**

Index   **206**

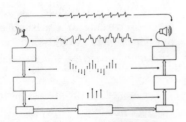

Preface

Voice technology does nothing more or less than allow us to talk to our machines, and they to us, with actual communication taking place. But this wouldn't be a worthwhile venture if this communication did nothing more than make for interesting novelties—chatty machines. Technological development consumes too much precious skilled labor time and too much money to waste on trivialities. There are so many important (and lucrative) areas awaiting the curious researcher and the venture capitalist (his partner in making things happen). Why should they invest their time, talent and money on voice technology? In the first chapter of this book you'll encounter enough reasons to last a lifetime. Yet, they all boil down to one underlying characteristic of voice technology—it is useful. This fact lies at the heart of all the current interest in the field.

This interest in speaking machines isn't all new, however. It only seems so because of the great advantages made over the last two years and the attention those technological strides have received. Documented research in voice technology dates back to the 1700s. Interest in speaking machines even ties in with ancient religions. Today it represents an extremely popular area for research.

Researchers choose the field because, in addition to being useful, voice technology is complex and compelling, intricate and interesting. In short, a challenge. And the challenge has drawn the attention of large investors. In April of 1980, the German corporation, Siemens, purchased 23.5 percent of Threshold Technology, a pioneer in practical speech-recognition equipment.

Threshold, in turn, has acquired its own integrated-circuit manufacturer, Auricle, Inc. Threshold expects that owning Auricle will reduce its equipment-construction costs and allow it to manufacture medium-priced equipment at a profit. The corporate goal is to accelerate the availability of low-cost speech-recognition equipment. According to Threshold's president, Dr. Thomas Martin, this equipment would find use in applications ranging from consumer products to peripherals for sophisticated computer systems.

Telesensory Systems got into the voice business by making talking calculators. Now, the firm's speech-product line has grown so fast that is has created a separate Speech Products Divison to handle the job. By spinning off the voice products, the firm hopes to accelerate and expand the commercialization of sophisticated speech-synthesis technology. Once again, a firm eyes an expanding market and intends to have products ready to open up that market.

One firm has carried more than its share of the load in popularizing and commercializing voice technology. Texas Instruments, Inc, manufacturer of the Speak & Spell, works hard to carry the idea of state-of-the-art technology to the consumer and industrial buyer alike. Now the firm has established an entire Speech Synthesis Technology Center to support its commitment to speech technology. Equipped with the latest in computer equipment, the speech center attacks problems ranging from new ways to put voices in consumer products to building complete voice-identification systems that will allow unmanned control entry to the nation's defense centers. And the range of products enjoys a certain amount of shared information. The more the firm learns about building toys that talk, the more they learn about how to identify a speaker's voice accurately.

Another firm looks toward the future and sees voice technology playing a major part. IBM has already developed hardware and software which indicate that the day of the voice-actuated typewriter—a machine which will take dictation—might be coming. You'll see the details of that research in the discussion on voice recognition (Chapter Five).

Bell Telephone has been purchasing voice-response systems for years. Now its own labs have created the prototype for a voice-controlled dialer—another potential voice product that could be ready for market in just a few years.

These examples of the products and research illustrate the scope of the efforts being put into developing voice technology. You can see that the large companies have joined (and in some cases begun) in the race to market with voice products. Yet, this remains an embryonic field. Even the nature of the research itself is still largely undefined.

The study of speech technology involves not one, but a multitude of disciplines. Sometimes called Speech Science, the field includes acoustics, linguistics, engineering, physiology, phonetics, statistics, communications theory, prosaics, forensics and semantics. If you enroll in the University of Southern California's doctoral degree program in Speech Science and Technology, you'll study all of these. And, before you can begin, you must have a Bachelor's degree in a related subject, such as anthropology, biological science, computer science, electrical engineering, mathematics, physics or one of the speech fields.

This degree program is unique. Although the Massachusetts Institude of Technology has offered related courses under the heading of speech communications, USC's program represents the only degree currently offered in the field. The next closest experience would involve working on one of the University projects which periodically emerge, delving into voice recognition.

Voice-output devices are already appearing in equipment, running the gamut from toys to jet fighters. As this is written, nearly every major automobile manufacturer is working on some sort of voice warning system to replace or augment the existing dashboard lights and gauges. The military implications of voice technology haven't been lost on the government. In December of 1977, the National Aeronautics and Space Administration (NASA), the Naval Training Equipment Center and the Naval Air Development Center put together a voice-technology symposium. The results were such that a new advisory group, affiliated with the Department of Defense Human Factors Engineering Technical Advisory Group, grew up. At the 1980 meeting in Dallas, TX, the keynote speaker, Dr. Walter LaBerge, Principle Deputy Under-Secretary of Defense, affirmed the government's interest in developing voice technology for the national defense.

Thus, it isn't difficult to predict that there is a voice input or output device (or both) in your future. Understanding the basics of voice technology will prepare you to understand the whys and wherefores of the next few generations of products. It has been said that the person who knows nothing of computers and programming is today's illiterate. Perhaps tomorrow it will be that person who doesn't understand the machines that he talks to and that talk to him. By understanding how they work, you can better use your tools. Understanding, then, helps make superior craftsmen.

Obviously, a single book can only scratch the surface of such a complex conglomerate of studies. This particular book promises simply to open the door to the basics of voice technology and illustrate the limitations and application of some of the current devices. We will look at state-of-the-art equipment and engineering techniques.

This book puts a special emphasis on voice equipment as peripheral equipment for computers. Voice data-entry equipment—nothing more than computers that accept spoken data—could represent a $1 billion business by 1990, and the technology that will create that market is being developed right now. Furthermore, voice devices are known as subsystems—they don't really do anything by themselves. The computer acts as a general-purpose device. A voice input or output device can do almost anything, given the right programming. Thus, by treating the whole system as a computer system, we create a general model that to some degree, applies to all applications.

Reading about a technology unhappily means learning a lot of new terms (buzzwords), and even new meanings for old terms. The glossary will help you cut through the muck and mire of speech technology's new language. Some terms are explain well enough in the text. If you get stuck, look to the glossary for help.

The appendices of a book should supply you with additional information too specific or detailed to be put into the text itself. Appendix A, therefore, points you to the most logical source of additional information—the equipment manufacturers. It is as complete a list as could be made at this time. Some of these are very large companies; others would hardly fill a garage. Their size, however, has little or nothing to do with the amount of help they can be. Some of the largest are surprisingly friendly; some of the smallest employ or are owned by extremely knowledgeable people. The text explains the nature of most of the companies' products—that should give you an idea of which ones you should contact for your needs.

A list of books comprises Appendix B. These are all good books, if by good you mean that they contain valuable information. Many of them, unfortunately, merely reprint technical papers, adding no annotation. These aren't especially clear or well written. After reading this book you should understand enough to be able to read the most convulated of technical papers on the subject, so read on.

Much of this book's material was developed for articles that appeared in *EDN* magazine (especially for the Special Report in the Nov. 20, 1979 issue). I would like to thank the entire *EDN* staff for their help, with a special thank you to Roy Foresberg, editorial director, Walt Patsone, editor, and Jordan Backler, managing editor.

Edward R. Teja

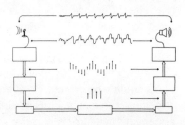

Chapter 1
Speech Recognition
And Synthesis—Why Bother?

Of the various design features that make up a product, the most exciting often has less to do with what that product is, or how it works, than how it interacts with people. It is people using products that give those products meaning. If something is easy to use it stands a better chance of being accepted than a product that does a better job but is difficult to use. Thus, product advertisements boast of their "ease of use." A product that appeals to our sense of whimsy also proves attractive. We want, not just products, but amusement as well. This explains the variety of packages that enclose rather similar products.

BUT IF IT COULD TALK

The work that goes into defining how the product will interact with its user is termed "human factors engineering." In the case of electronic engineering, this concern deals with the man-machine interface—the way the operator will have to use the devices. This includes determining the amount of operator training required to use the device as well as where to put the knobs.

The task of human engineering even includes considering the psychology of using the device. Engineers must ask "how will the user perceive the device? Will it be welcomed or considered an invasion into human prerogatives?" This is why so many computer systems come with what the trade calls *friendly* software. Friendly software is really nothing more than computer programs written such that the user feels comfortable using the machine. The operator has been taken into account.

The difference between conventional programs and friendly ones becomes most obvious when you look at the program's prompts—the words that tell the operator what to do next. These instructions used to be nothing more than a cryptic symbol, such as a question mark. When companies began selling systems to people who couldn't be expected to know in advance how to use the machines, the manufacturers elaborated a little. But just a little. The second software generation might print:

NAME?

for example. Today's friendly programs, intended to appeal to a much wider audience, might print out:

PLEASE ENTER YOUR FULL NAME, LAST NAME FIRST

This made the operator feel like part of the system, rather than an incompetent beginner. Yet, no amount of good programming gets around the inescapable fact that not everyone feels comfortable using a keyboard. People who aren't used to using a keyboard to communicate with machinery won't be convinced that it is necessary. If you want to sell to this market—a much larger market than the existing buyers—you need a method to make the hardware, not just the software, friendly. After all, if they won't use the hardware, they'll never find out what a good job you did making the software easy to use.

Computers and voice technology provide one good and friendly answer to the man-machine interface problem. It adapts the machines to the people who will use them instead of expecting the people to take up touch typing to operate the machines. It requires a minimum of operator training—people spend their entire lives learning, with varying success, how to communicate through speech. A little friendly software can guide the operator through the entire sequence of events needed to run the machine—whatever it is. All the human does, then, is make the decisions and supply data. The machine does all the work. Isn't that why machines were invented, after all?

Speaking to a machine is much like speaking to someone who hasn't been speaking your language very long. You must think about speaking clearly, and sometimes speak slower than normal. But that's with the current generation of voice-input equipment. Improvements are on the way that may make even these small concessions to machinery unnecessary.

And this comprises just the beginning of what voice input and output can do for humans. The dream of every voice-technology researcher goes far beyond just making existing machinery easy to use. The dream views new machines that can make people more efficient in everything they do, machines that will favorably impact the way we live.

The prospect of using voice control in our everyday lives has such widespread potential that some manufacturers have improved sales simply by adding voice-actuated switches to otherwise ordinary products. This doesn't constitute voice control, of course. Any loud acoustic noise within the speech bandwidth will usually trigger such a device. But the interest on the part of consumers has not been lost on marketing managers.

True voice control comprises control over a device's functions to the extent that you would have if you stood in front of the device and operated it with switches and knobs. Voice control includes both the ability to command an action and to indicate the degree of the command. It isn't enough, for example, to be able to turn on a radio by saying "on." You must also be able to tune the radio and set the volume and tone controls by voice. Otherwise you really haven't gained any practical advantage.

And voice control isn't the only aspect of voice technology that has begun showing its commercial potential. Appliances and toys that can talk can use this ability to sell themselves—literally. And today these products have begun arriving. The boxes in stores that used to blink colored lights at us, now offer to correct our spelling and ensure that the roast in the oven will be cooked to perfection—if we will just tell them how we want it done.

Although much of the spotlight has stayed on verbal toys as they have been introduced, there are other areas which have shown remarkable progress as well. True, Toshiba's talking microwave oven and voice-controlled television set, first shown in Japan, demand a great deal of attention. Panasonic's talking clock radio, shown in Fig. 1-1, points out another use for today's speech chips. Nor is Panasonic the only firm selling talking radios. Omnicron Electronics Corp markets a talking clock for industrial use. The clock, shown in Fig. 1-2, will log the time on magnetic tape whenever a time announcement is called for. The $385 unit speaks in a clear male voice. A built-in battery backup prevents the clock from failing just because the power company lets you down.

This industrial-strength clock illustrates that the real technology push is toward, not just chatty toys, but tools that will help make us more productive, more efficient. Verbal control over our machines can increase our productivity. Voice control and voice-response systems make the control we exercise over our

Fig. 1-1. Panasonic's Model RC5800 talking clock radio.

machines more immediate than that which push-button systems provide. Voice prompting—the machine cueing the operator—sets the stage for machines whose entire operating manual exists in software only. The machine gives directions on how to operate it properly.

Look at the world of the business office. Office automation has become big business, and voice will play an increasingly significant role. At IBM, research indicates that typewriters that take dictation might be in our future. Being able to generate letters, memos and forms at 180 words per minute might mean an end to one large component of secretarial drudge work that takes up valuable human skills. In a day of secretarial shortages, the value of such a machine can't be easily overrated.

The products that use voice technology apply it for differing reasons. Although some manufacturers obviously hope that voice technology will give their products sufficient novelty to sell extra units, many have turned to voice communication because of its efficiency. No other means of communication even comes close. Because speech comes naturally to adults (we've trained in this technique most of our lives), we're less likely to make mistakes when speaking (and listening) than when communicating through a typewriter keyboard or other mechanical data-entry method. Furthermore, vocal communication lets you perform complex tasks requiring both hands and eyes at the same time you are entering data into a computer.

An audible alarm attracts more attention than does a blinking light, and it can alert an operator to a problem in equipment that is out of sight. An alarm that is both audible and intelligent—a vocal alert—can make the operator's response more efficient by providing information on the nature of the failure or emergency. A voice saying "drill press number five is on fire" gives the operator an idea of what he faces before he even reaches the equipment. Such a vocal alert could even telephone the fire department automatically if not overridden by the operator within a certain period of time.

National Semiconductor estimates that by 1982 cars will come equipped with speech synthesizers connected to their warning gauges to take advantage of the benefits of vocal alerts. At the 1980 Society of Automotive Engineers Congress and Exposition in Detroit, the firm demonstrated a prototype automotive diagnostic warning system that might prove the wave of the future. This synthesizer system takes inputs from a microcontroller and gives audible warnings such as low fuel, low brake fluid, door open, fasten seat belts and others. Such synthesizer can help reduce the confusion produced by flashing lights and gauges. A European manufacturer, VDO, is reportedly working on its own system for cars. Given VDO's expertise with automobile instrumentation, it will be interesting to see how this firms's approach differs from National Semiconductor's.

The concept of reducing indicator confusion is not a trivial one. Some situations, such as flying an aircraft, demand nearly all of an operator's attention—and both hands. Yet the operator can't afford to lose touch with the status of the aircraft's performance.

Fig. 1-2. Omnicron's talking clock records the time for you.

The simplest solution thus far is one analogous to that of National Semiconductor's car unit. In fact, at least one manufacturer has marketed a talking altimeter for several years now. Voice technology can also contribute to the controlling end of things. Remember that the pilot literally has his hands full. Adding a voice-input unit that could carry out noncritical jobs while the operator concentrates on the important ones makes the task of flying somewhat more manageable. In jet fighters the task of flying has grown so complex that, as the weapons system demands more of the pilot's attention, flying skills actually deteriorate. There's a limit to the number of similar tasks (such as reading dials) that any person can do well simultaneously. Replacing the variety of bells, tones and buzzers used to indicate status of equipment, with verbal messages that are coordinated to relate to specific problems, would reduce the pilot's visual work load. He wouldn't have to scan the instruments quite so often.

Voice technology helps pilots train for flying too. Simulators can be made simpler with voice-response systems acting as air controllers. The trainer's operator, faced with many of the same problems that the pilot faces, can be made to work more efficiently with voice technology.

In factories, inspectors examining units must pick them up, examine them, set them down, write down any defects noted (or that there were no defects) and then move the unit to the next bin. Voice-input technology lets the inspector enter this information while inspecting the unit. Any defects are noted as they are found. Each piece gets picked up only once.

In the manual system it might take four people to complete the inspection process and prepare the reports. At each step in the process numbers can be inadvertently changed. A voice system enters the data directly into the host computer. Keypunch errors and transcription errors never get a chance to creep into the system.

Threshold Technology has installed inspection systems for Continental Can (in 1974) and Reynolds Metals (in 1976). Combining voice input with a prompting display that keeps the operator up to date on where he is in his inspection process and what information the system expects next, these firms established efficient can-lid inspection stations that provide strict control over the acquired data. Continental Can's operation has proven so efficient that the firm's industrial engineers estimate that the voice system has increased each inspection's throughput by 40 percent.

TALKING DATABASES

A talking computer can help a firm keep track of its inventory and provide accurate recordkeeping, even when the operators don't have direct access to a video terminal and data modem. At the Penn-Jersey Regional Red Cross Blood Center, based in Philadelphia, a talking computer helps ensure that whole blood doesn't get wasted. Whole blood must be used within 21 days of its collection or it becomes ineffective for transfusions. At $20 per pint it doesn't take much spoilage before hospitals begin to look to computers to help them keep track of their stock.

This particular system accepts information on blood use from 43 area hospitals. The central computer knows which hospitals have which blood. The hospital officials enter data on a regular basis.

The cost of equipping each of the 43 hospitals with terminals and modems would be great. Because this system can talk, however, this equipment is unnecessary. The hospital official simply enters data with a push-button telephone. A decoder at the computer accepts the tones and converts them to ASCII characters. Then, most importantly, the computer repeats the data so that the operator can be sure the data has been entered properly.

If the computer didn't have a voice of its own, there would be no way—short of buying data-entry equipment—that the hospital personnel could access the database directly. They would either have to fill in forms to a data-processing division where the information would be, belatedly, entered, or forget the whole thing. But the computer's voice and tone decoders turn any push-button telephone into a data-entry terminal. How well does the system work? Votrax, the computer voice's manufacturer, reports that since the system's installation, blood loss due to spoilage has dropped from 19 percent to 5.7 percent.

The same advantages that make the talking computer suitable for monitoring the blood bank's inventory also work in other applications. In 1977, General Motors announced a system designed to aid dealers in finding out whether or not a particular car was in need of recall work. Thus, when a car came in for service, the dealer could pick up a telephone, enter the car's identification number with the push-button pad and find out if it needed work. Once again, without giving the computer a voice, it would be impossible for a dealer to access the information database directly. And delays in processing the information would make the system useless.

Gulf Coast Automotive Warehouse Co. bought a computerized voice-response system to ensure quick response for 60 auto-parts stores in the Houston, TX area. Transcom provided terminals allowing the stores to connect directly to the computer and effectively generate their own shipping voucher. In its first three and one-half months of operation, one store owner estimated it had saved his store three weeks' work.

A national network of approximately 3700 Lincoln-Mercury auto dealers use an audio data terminal to connect to Ford's Direct Order Entry System. Each dealer calls the nearest parts distribution center where a voice-response system (voice by Cognitronics' 682 Speechmaker) takes his order. The audio response tells the dealer the status of the order as soon as he has entered it.

Although both of these systems require terminals to enter data into the system, they still illustrate the idea of entering data over normal telephone lines. The voice, in both cases, helps ensure the accuracy of the data and provide natural, concise prompts that make sure the operator enters the data correctly and has the correct numbers.

DEDICATED SUPPLIERS

You'll find the number of suppliers of voice equipment increasing dramatically as the technology matures. Those in the business today have broken the ground and made the idea of products using voice technology acceptable to the general public. They have invested the time and effort because they foresee a market of giant proportions. In a speech to his company's stockholders, Texas Instruments, Inc.'s president, Fred Bucy, said that speech synthesis is "one of the most exciting innovations in interface technology since the development of the cathode-ray tube."

Mr. Bucy's firm is, of course, one of the leaders in bringing voice technology to market. TI's Speak & Spell (Fig. 1-3) pioneered low-cost voice-output devices for the consumer market. The Speak & Spell's acceptance laid the groundwork for future consumer products. After all, if your kid's toys can talk it doesn't seem so unusual to think about talking microwaves, refrigerators and dishwashers.

TI's commitment to voice technology is enormous, and not restricted to gadgets for the consumer market. They use voice technology themselves. In cooperation with various government groups, the firm has developed a voice-identification system that controls access to restricted areas. Nowadays, to get into TI's computer center without an escort requires that the computer know who you are by the sound of your voice. In an anteroom leading into the computer center, the door locks behind you, and you are asked to repeat a phrase that the computer generates from its vocabulary. This vocabulary comprises words that persons qualified to enter the center have already repeated for the computer during a training process. The computer selects words randomly from the vocabulary to prevent an unauthorized intruder from simply tape recording an authorized person's voice and playing the tape for the computer.

Fig. 1-3. Even electronic games can have a voice (courtesy of Texas Instrument Inc.).

The random word selection means that the sentences don't always make much sense—but the point is only to identify the speaker, not generate literary gems. If after a few tries the computer doesn't recognize the speaker, it automatically calls the security guard to find out who is in the anteroom.

The system isn't perfected yet. At least not such that it could be sold commercially. Each installation requires too much fine tuning and costs far too much. But the market is there when the systems are.

HELPING THE HANDICAPPED

Voice technology finds special application in helping the handicapped use machinery to put them on a par with other people. Cerebral palsy, multiple sclerosis, mental disorders and injuries to the head and neck can all impair a person's ability to communicate effectively. In looking at what such people need from technologists, Votrax found evidence that although no one device would serve the needs of all vocally impaired people, almost all of them preferred a means that would let them communicate orally. The firm's tests indicated that symbols, lights, movements and signs just don't provide as effective communication as do oral communicators.

Tests also indicated that, to serve the needs of the most people, the communicator would have to be easy to use, small, portable, safe, versatile and durable.

The Phonic Mirror Handivoice, shown in Fig. 1-4, proved to be Votrax's answer to solving the problems of oral communication. The device comprises three basic parts: a speech synthesizer, a speaker and a command device. For handicapped persons who have medium to maximum motor capabilities and high cognitive skills, Votrax provides the unit with a calculator keyboard. You type in a 3-digit word that corresponds to a word, phrase or sentence stored in the synthesizer. You can store up to 40 of these 3-digit codes before making the synthesizer speak. A single keystroke will repeat the entire stored message.

For handicapped persons without the motor skills necessary to operate a keyboard, the manufacturer provides auxiliary activator devices such as a throat pickup. One sound made in the throat would cause an electronic scanning alphabet board to begin scanning. The board indicates the letters of the alphabet, one at a time. By making a throat noise when the appropriate letter is indicated, the user selects the desired entry.

This key-scanning scheme has its own problems, however. Users get frustrated and tired when entering long letter sentences. Thus, a vocabulary board was designed to make entry easier. With this vocabulary board, the user can enter an entire word with a single touch. Divided into 120 touch-sensitive blocks, the board provides a 480-word vocabulary. A menu of four word choices is available in each block.

Another class of handicapped people are also served by voice technology. The blind can already communicate verbally well enough, but require Braille translations of books and other printed material unless they have someone to read to them. Furthermore,

Fig. 1-4. Handivoice helps the vocally impaired communicate (courtesy of Votrax).

information stored in computers has, until recently, been all but inaccessible to the blind.

The problem of printed matter is being solved by machines such as Kurzweil Computer Products' Reading Machine, shown in Fig. 1-5. It makes this information directly available to the blind by reciting the text out loud. Any printed matter placed on its surface will be read. Widely accepted in libraries, the Reading Machine is still too expensive for individual ownership, but advancing technology will solve that problem too.

Telesensory Systems, Inc, has a long record of building viable enabling technology—devices that aid the handicapped. Quick to see the advantages of speech technology in building these devices, TSI pioneered speech modules for use in calculators. The firm's Speech Plus talking calculator offers a 24-word vocabulary that also provides an 8-digit readout. The six-function calculator comes in English, French, German and Arabic for under $400.

TSI has marketed a device called the Optacon Print Reading System for some time now. This system converts regular print into an enlarged vibrating tactile form. To read text, the blind person moves a miniature camera across a line of print with the right hand. The left index finger sits on the Optacon's tactile array. As the camera moves across the letter, the image is reproduced on the array.

Now TSI has combined its experience with Optacon with its speech knowhow to produce a voice-output reading system. Under a grant from the Veterans' Administration, TSI is establishing several test sites to aid in the last-stage development of the reading system.

The last area of information that was inaccessible to the blind resided in computers. The same technology that makes it practical for a calculator to talk, or for a machine to read a book aloud, also removes this last restriction. What better location for a computer voice than inside a computer terminal? And that's exactly where Maryland Computer Services put one. The Total Talk System (Fig. 1-6) provides the obvious, but uncommon, function of reading aloud what is presented on its display screen. Beneficial in both vocational and educational settings, these talking devices let the blind compete with sighted persons on an equal footing. Furthermore, giving the blind direct access to private material through the use of these machines helps ensure them a privacy that wasn't available before.

Fig. 1-5. A desktop reading machine (courtesy of Kurzweil Computer Products).

Installations intended for the handicapped might well prove to make everyone more efficient. At the University of Kentucky, Maryland Computer Services installed a talking telephone directory (TTD) for a blind operator, Robin McFarland. The equipment, designed to make her more efficient, worked so well that she was

Fig. 1-6. A Total Talk terminal (courtesy of Maryland Computer Services Inc.).

soon handling 85 calls per hour. Her sighted counterparts, using conventional retrieval methods, handled only 50 to 55 calls per hour.

And you don't have to be blind to use the system, and thus increase your call throughput. Anyone who can type a name on a keyboard will hear that person's phone number spoken in about six seconds. Because the system also displays the information on its screen, the deaf aren't penalized either.

TALK TO MACHINES

The struggle to market products and systems employing voice technology has no definite beginning and end. But it's fair to say that the development of voice-input technology is still in its infancy. Yet, voice-input systems already available hint a revolution in the way we handle information. Voice-input progressed so rapidly between 1978 and 1980 that even the experts were caught off guard. The technology has grown from science fiction speculation to industrial reality.

Wilson Foods, for example, enters data on incoming hogs into a computer. The firm uses voice technology to enter the data directly to the computer. If the system hasn't completely paid for itself within two years, Wilson Foods will be surprised.

If you let your bank pay your bills for you, through one of the new pay-by-phone schemes, you might be talking to a computer on a regular basis already. In the same way that the blood bank's order-entry systems discussed earlier took advantage of telephones to enter data directly into the computer, banks are turning to the telephone for funds transfer. It's not unreasonable to give customers direct access to the computer in a controlled manner via the telephone.

Verbex Corporation has taken this procedure one step further, however. Verbex's system, shown in Fig. 1-7, lets you say the digits rather than enter them with a push-button keypad. This minor improvement might sound simple; yet, as you'll see in detail in Chapter Five, taking this step involved a giant technological effort.

The benefit of voice input is that you cannot only use an ordinary telephone as a computer terminal—helping avoid costly and confusing data-entry errors—but you can enter the data with your hands full and with a standard dial telephone.

The Hueristics' Model 7000 voice terminal, shown in Fig. 1-8, illustrates the hands-free operation of voice data entry—and its advantage. The technician shown in the photo has both hands available to make critical adjustments safely and accurately. Yet, at any point in his work, he can enter detailed information about the unit he is working on.

And voice control is beginning to appear in sophisticated systems such as computer-automated design systems. Calma Company has introduced a 50-word voice-control unit (Fig. 1-9) that accepts single-word commands or phrases up to one second long. Its 99.8 percent accuracy makes for efficient hands-free control. Using the headset shown, the operator can perform all of the Vector Memory Display functions, including continuous pan, zoom, multiple view and composite image under voice command.

Fig. 1-7. The Model 1800 System lets anyone talk to a computer (courtesy of Verbex Corporation).

Fig. 1-8. The Heuristics 7000 system allows hands-free data entry (courtesy of Heuristics Inc.).

LEARNING TO SPEAK SPEECH

Short of getting a job in a speech-research laboratory or taking a college degree program in speech technology, is there any way to learn enough about speech technology to put it to good use? Absolutely. The growing interest in speech technology has spawned several significant seminars on the subject. In addition to irregular sessions held by Wayne Lea (889 Sanford Court, Santa Barbara, CA 93111) on computer recognition of speech, a number of professional instruction companies are now offering schedules of classes. Integrated Computer Systems, for example, offers a Voice Input/Output course at various locations across the country. The course includes extensive demonstrations of voice equipment. You can get a complete schedule of classes by writing the company at 3304 Pico Boulevard, Santa Monica, CA 90405.

The Technology Transfer Institute (Box 49765, Los Angeles, CA 90049) has introduced a three-day seminar called *Machines that Understand Speech*. This one focuses on the recognition aspects of voice technology.

These courses and seminars aren't cheap. Instead, they are a cost-effective way to learn. The Technology Transfer Institute courses, for example, run $675. Considering the information density you'll find, and the fact that your sources of information are still a bit restricted, the price is quite reasonable.

Fig. 1-9. Recognizing your spoken commands makes Calma's Computer Aided Design System an effective tool.

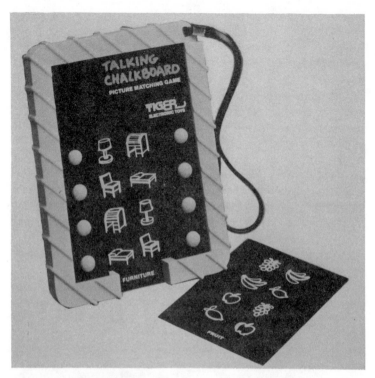

Fig. 1-10. Speech makes learning tools, such as Tiger Electronic Toys' Talking Chalkboard more effective.

Don't overlook the manufacturers themselves as a source of information and education—especially if you are planning to purchase some of the more expensive equipment or commit your company to large quantities of a single-source speech chip. Most firms offer some form of classroom instruction on their equipment. Interstate Electronics Corp., for example, provides a three-day workshop on its voice-recognition module (VRM) that is part sales pitch and mostly solid applications engineering knowhow.

If the history of microcomputer manufacturers can serve as any sort of guide, the trend is toward more educational opportunities. The manufacturers realize that knowledge, about the technology and the products, will sell hardware and software. Getting informed, therefore, should become easier and easier. Workshops and seminars will spring up all over.

Texas Instruments has taken a slightly different approach to helping customers. Rather than concentrate on classes, the firm has built regional speech centers all over the country. Specialists at these centers can then focus their attention on helping manufacturers solve specific speech-output problems. They don't teach speech, but the information is indirectly available. A speech center won't help you if you don't know what questions to ask, however.

Perhaps the ultimate solution lies in a combination of approaches. It isn't hard to visualize engineers taking some speech technology during their formal education, going to seminars to brush up before attacking a new design task, and using speech centers (or some equivalent) to get design-specific tips and assistance.

Each manufacturer will find its own best way of helping you understand the proper and practical use of its equipment. In the meantime, examine the courses, and get out to see the equipment.

Fig. 1-11. A Talking Picturebook employs phoneme synthesis.

Fig. 1-12. The Learning Computer talks to make its point.

32

Many of the larger firms demonstrate the equipment at trade and computer shows all over the country. Calma, for example, introduced its voice-input unit at a show in Dallas. If you went to the Consumer Electronics Show in Las Vegas in 1981, you might have seen one of the latest examples of the current sophistication of voice-output equipment. Tiger Electronic Toys introduced an entire line of talking toys, including learning tools such as the Talking Chalkboard (Fig. 1-10) , the Talking Picturebook (Fig. 1-11) and the Talking Learning Computer (Fig. 1-12). These learning toys apply computer and voice technology to the problems of teaching. The Talking Learning Computer, for example, teaches mathematics, spelling and reading. It applies its 1500-word vocabulary to the task in 15 different learning modes, each mode having its own educational goals. The technology that makes this toy (tool) possible isn't exotic or futuristic. In fact, you'll read all about it in this book, although because of its proprietary nature we won't dissect the Tiger Electronic Toys. But you should be able to figure out the chips and technology that the manufacturer applied.

But the best way to see what voice technology can do is to get involved in making it happen. Make your learning experience one of exploration. Get the equipment and work with it; design your own voice equipment; go to manufacturer's demonstrations; watch for new applications of voice technology and try to see how they do what they do. It is involvement that gives you an edge in understanding the technology.

One of the delightful qualities of voice technology is its pioneering atmosphere. Nearly any approach is fair game. Nearly any application is suitable for voice input and output until the experience proves otherwise. This barnstorming air, along with good research, makes for an exciting area of work. Besides, talking to a computer for the first time can be a strange feeling.

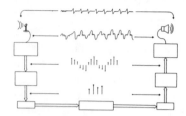

Chapter 2
The Speech Process

Understanding the way in which we perceive speech, the manner by which we communicate through sound waves, proves difficult. The recognition of sound waves as speech requires some of the most complex concepts involved in artificial intelligence. You'll get a better idea of that task when we deal with the recognizers later on.

Even isolating this discussion to the act of producing speech doesn't make it simple. There are so many factors contributing to the meaning of a sound wave that we can't control the speech process consciously. We have to depend on our reflexes to convert our intended communication into acoustic waves. This means not only manipulating the vocal tract to produce the right words, but also ensuring that inflection, intonation and tone are correct. When we don't do this properly, people say, "Why are you talking to me in that tone of voice?" You see, these other factors can impart as much, or even more, meaning, than the words themselves.

THE SOUNDS OF SPEECH

We can begin our discussion about speech with information about the basic sounds we use to communicate. The people who describe the speech sounds work in a field called *phonetics*. When they begin looking at groupings of the sounds, they are studying *phonematics*. Both fields look at *phonemes*, the basic speech sounds. When you combine phonemes so that they have meaning, you have created a *morpheme*. If you modify a phoneme's character slightly, you have created an *allophone*.

Although you can analyze any language in terms of its phonemes, both their number and nature vary from language to language. A language can contain as few as two vowel phonemes or as many as 12. Languages are known to use anywhere from a dozen consonant phonemes to 60 or 70.

English has aproximately 40 vowel and consonant phonemes together. The exact numbers vary with the expert you talk to . You see, the task of deciding whether a sound is the result of one basic sound or two other basic sounds combined can become quite subjective. And it's hard to say if there's a correct answer at all. Or even if it matters.

When two words are very close, you stand the greatest chance of confusing the two. Look at the words "bat" and "sat," for example. They differ in sound by only one phoneme. These words are called a minimally distinct pair. The situation can get worse, too. Consider the problem of separating "bat" from "pat." Now the difference between the two is still one phoneme, and there isn't much difference between the two phonemes. In this case, we call the problem minimally distinct phonemes.

UNDERSTANDING WHAT WAS MEANT

One problem facing researchers of computerized speech communication is that the human brain is capable of understanding what was meant even if the speaker doesn't speak clearly or completely. Suppose a friend walks up and says quite clearly "go mor." This makes no sense at all written down. If the sounds are the only ones received, however, then they are all you have to work with. Fortunately, your brain has access to information that can put things in proper perspective.

The first thing that your brain might add to the information bank is that the speaker is a friend. This might be deduced by sight or tone of voice. Nonetheless, it is added. This suggests that the message, being the first one of the day, might be a friendly greeting. That information alone reduces the number of possible matches.

If you also know that the message was received during the morning, the brain quickly makes the proper match, and you "hear" the phrase "good morning" instead of the sounds actually spoken.

This is the area that artificial intelligence has yet to conquer. Developing a method of giving the intelligence access to all this possibly related, possibly irrelevant information in the hope of improving recognition requires an organization technique we don't have yet. Not on that scale, at least.

The process of examining several, not necessarily related, bits of information at the same time can take place because of the brain's ability to act as a parallel processor. It processes several tasks simultaneously. As you'll see in Chapter Five, the task of recognizing and responding to speech (by machines) finds limits in the availability of computer manufacturers to provide parallel processing capability. Even at IBM, experimental results indicate that what is needed to perform reasonable transcriptions of speech—to do a task which people perform daily—will require more sophisticated computer technology.

Even with more powerful computers, the task of making machines communicate with the means most natural to humans— speech—remains formidable. This is in part because the first job of any designer of a voice input or output device is always to specify that which will be produced or accepted. Dr. G. Fant of the Institute of Telegraphy and Telephony, Royal Institute of Technology, Stockholm, Sweden, pointed out that even though today's recording and analysis techniques make it possible to specify the speech wave fairly accurately, a detailed description would prove unmanageable. "The great problem," he wrote, "is to find useful approximation."

Although Dr. Gant wrote these words in 1959, the message is true today. All voice input and output devices must work from models that employ "useful approximations" of the real thing. Dr. Gant summed the problem up succinctly when he wrote, "The neurophysiology of speaking and hearing are the least accessible links of the complete communication system but they carry the key to many interesting problems."

THE PHYSICS OF SPEECH

Speaking actually occurs as a byproduct of respiration. When the airflow from the lungs to the mouth is unobstructed, no sound is made at all. You are simply breathing. By introducing obstructions into that path you produce longitudinal vibrations—acoustic waves. If you control the introduction of obstructions, such as placement of the tongue, you can control the sounds. Speech is a sophisticated form of that control.

Your vocal tract, shown in Fig. 2-1, acts as a time-varying filter that changes the resonant characteristics of the air's path. Your control over the various obstructions determines your control over your speech. People with speech handicaps are, quite simply, people who, for one reason or another, have no control over one or more of their vocal tract's elements. This lack of control keeps them from being able to produce the full range of speech sounds.

Figure 2-2 illustrates a block diagram of the entire system. The vocal chords can cause the airflow to oscillate, affecting the way the later obstructions will produce sounds. If you constrict the airflow (compress or draw together the path's obstructions to reduce the size of the available opening) at some point, you'll produce what is termed a fricative sound. Fricatives actually comprise the sound of the turbulence caused by eddy currents around the obstruction. This technique produces such sounds as sh, zh and th. Completely closing off the airpath, building air pressure up behind the closure (which might be the lips and teeth) and then abruptly releasing the trapped air, produces a plosive sound. A plosive usually has fricative noise following it. This illustrates how the articulators can influence the sound's production.

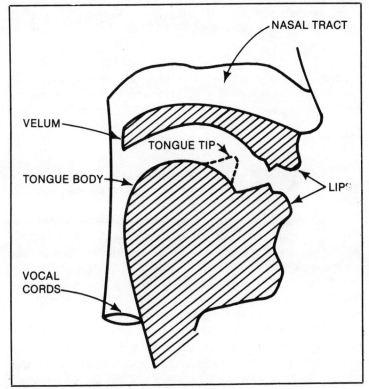

Fig. 2-1. A cross section of the human vocal tract.

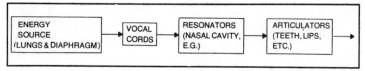

Fig. 2-2. A block diagram of the speech system.

WHERE YOU SAY IT

Selecting where sounds are made affects the actual sound that will be made. This is referred to as the process of articulation. Articulation implies both how you say words and:

☐ the point in the vocal tract that you close off or constrict
☐ the amount of airflow that you cut off or constrict.

Choosing the proper place to articulate a word makes a greater difference in that word's intelligibility than you might imagine at first. But, if you remember that the tract is a resonant cavity, the effect of moving the articulation point makes more sense. By relocating the articulation point a little bit, you change the size of more than one cavity.

Think about the way you say an "f," for example. Is it possible to pronounce the sound without letting your lower lip nearly (or completely) touch your upper front teeth? This touching is termed labiodental articulation and is one of the articulation forms that can be seen by an observer. Such visible articulation makes lip reading possible. Watch yourself in a mirror as you say the letters "f" and "v." If you speak them clearly, you should observe labiodental articulation.

Another visible articulation, bilabial articulation, produces the sounds "b," "p" or "m." As its Latin name suggests, bilabial means that the two lips come together.

The invisible (or at least less visible) articulations appear in producing dental sounds. If you touch your tongue to the back of your teeth, you can produce a "th" sound. Moving your tongue back, along the roof of your mouth, you come to a bump called the alveolar ridge. Touch your tongue to this point and you produce "t", "d" and "s." You can move your tongue back even further in your mouth to make retroflexive sounds—"r" and "er."

At each of the articulation points, notice that you had the possibility of making at least two different sounds. This difference lies in how the acoustic wave had been shaped before it reached the articulation point. One large distinction in sounds lies between voiced and unvoiced sounds. Voiced sounds are those made with the vocal cords vibrating; in unvoiced sounds they are still. The "b," for example, is a voiced sound, whereas its articulation partner "p" is unvoiced. You can feel the difference in your larynx when you say these two.

SPEECH PARAMETERS

An acoustic signal comprises several characteristics that we can examine separately, including:

- [ ] loudness
- [ ] duration
- [ ] timing
- [ ] pitch
- [ ] timbre

Thus, it would work reasonably well to categorize acoustic signals according to some rating system for each of these qualities. You could even analyze these characteristics and infer what letter had been spoken (with fair accuracy) by measuring them. Yet, speech is much more complex a structure than simply the production of isolated sounds. As mentioned earlier, we encode our speech by the way we say things as well as by the words we choose to use. The techniques we use, both consciously and unconsciously, to add extra meaning to our speech are termed *prosodic features*.

The term prosodic refers to any characteristic that lasts longer than one phoneme. It includes long-term variations in speech features, such as the voice's pitch. Other prosodic features include stress patterns (whether you accent the first or last syllable, for example) and the rate at which you speak. Dr. Wayne Lea, at the Speech Communications Research Laboratory in Los Angeles, California, has even discovered that the time interval between stressed syllables affects the particular manner in which you say those sounds. If two stressed syllables come close together you will say them quite differently than if they are separated by several unstressed syllables. An interesting sidelight to this phenomenon is that the faster you speak, the worse you speak. Speaking fast forces the stressed syllables closes together and causes speech problems to degenerate.

PUTTING SOUNDS TOGETHER

The fact that we talk differently at different speaking rates points up another speech problem. *You never say a sound in a word the same way you'd say that sound by itself.* While you are forming each sound with your mouth and vocal tract, your brain must be planning how to say the next sound. Furthermore, you had to move the articulators and other speech paraphernalia from some previous position (exactly where depends on the previous sound). During normal speech, you'll typically change the way you say the current sound to accommodate the next sound coming up, and the current sound is also modified slightly by the lingering effects of having just made the previous sound. So you see that the sounds that come just before and just after the sound you are trying to make both play a role in how you say a sound. The effect is called coarticulation. You are trying to articulate all three sounds over time, not just one. This is, to a large extent, why speech models are time-varying filters.

Another factor that changes as you talk is loudness. Loudness is a measurement of the stress you give to a word and it affects the word's meaning in that context. Stress can indicate that the end of a sentence has been reached, or that the sentence is a question. To convince yourself that you do change the stress of sounds, depending on the context, try saying the words "nitrate" and "night rate" consecutively.

According to a 1931 *Bell System Technical Journal*, " . . . all of the fundamental sounds that contribute to the loudness of speech," are contained in the sentences: "Joe took father's shoe bench out," and "she was waiting at my lawn."

You can't really separate the effects of loudness and coarticulation. The worse the coarticulation effects are, the more they'll change the stresses. This is partly the explanation for the clarity of short, simple sentences in plays. Long, complex sentences can become lost in total unintelligibilty.

A MODEL SPEAKER

Engineers like to build models. Building models helps them better understand something that is too complex to play with directly. Various modeling attempts have been applied to speech to overcome the difficulties pointed out by Dr. Gant.

The block diagram shown in Fig. 2-3 presents an engineer's idea of the functional model of a speech mechanism. This model, in fact, represents how Texas Instruments views speech in constructing its speech chips. The use of two descriptions allows defining the speech signal in terms of how it acts over time and at each frequency of interest. Each of the spectral peaks shown could represent what is termed a format—a frequency band containing

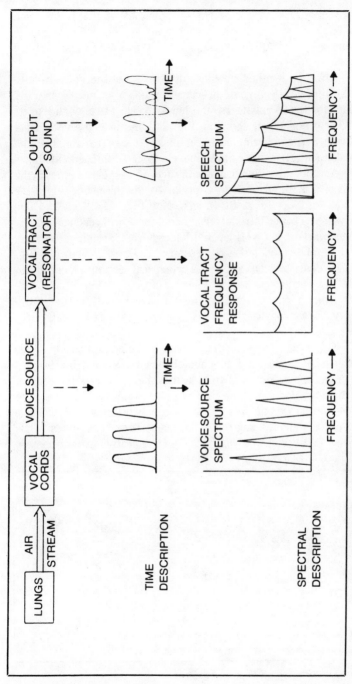

Fig. 2-3. The vocal tract as a time-varying filter (courtesy of Texas Instruments Inc.).

41

more energy than its neighbors. Synthesizing a male voice speaking a normal English vowel would require three basic formats—one at 200 to 800 Hz, one at 900 to 2300 Hz and the third at 2400 to 3000 Hz.

A format synthesizer looks at a model of the vocal tract to determine how you could produce any given sound electrically. Thus, for these engineers, the human vocal tract looks like its electrical equivalent shown in Fig. 2-4. Because the vocal tract acts as a time-varying filter, it makes sense to translate the vocal-tract's element positions into electrical filter coefficients.

Another attempt to capture the actions of speech comes in the form of a mathematical description. At the 38th meeting of the Acoustical Society at St. Louis, Nov. 18, 1949, H.K. Dunn presented a paper introducing a model for vowel resonances. Dr. Dunn, who did his work at Bell Laboratories, assumed the vocal tract could be modeled as two resonant cavities. as shown in Fig. 2-5. He described it as a series of cylindrical sections placed end to end. The piston represents the source of air at the vocal cords. The four cylinders represent (1) the throat cavity, (2), the mouth cavity, (3) a constriction due to the lips and (4) a baffle that acts as the speaker's face.

This rough model worked accurately enough that Dr. Dunn and his colleagues at Bell Laboratories were able, in 1950, to produce an electric vocal tract at the Massachusetts Institute of Technology for the Speech Communication Conference. The device produced only vowels and needed work, but it served as a model for standardizing the definition of vowel phonemes. Thus the model served to give speech-communications researchers a

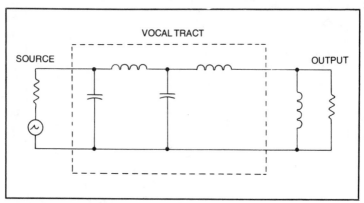

Fig. 2-4. The electrical equivalent of the vocal tract.

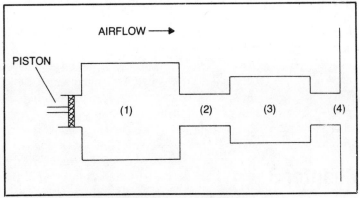

Fig. 2-5. Bell Laboratories' two-tube resonance model.

tool to investigate the way we speak and to represent their findings.

As you see, the way we speak isn't entirely known. Today we have better models—refinements of the old models—that allow research to progress, but our knowledge of how the brain coordinates all this parallel activity (there's that concept again) isn't clear.

Some early synthesizers tried to duplicate the physical nature of the speech process, with varying results. In 1791, Wolfgang Von Kempelen built an apparatus that generated connected utterances. He connected a bellows to a reed which excited a hand-controlled resonator. The operator controlled four separate constricted passages with the hand that wasn't controlling the resonator. The limit of such a mechanical device usually lies in the ability of the operator to coax subtle speech sounds from it. In this sense, the speaking machine isn't operated as a machine, but played in the manner of a musical instrument. Thus, there's a fairly long training time before an operator could manage anything resembling speech.

Futhermore, any mechanical speaker faces a difficulty faced by any speaking person—the problems of coarticulation. Unfortunately, you usually have less control over a machine than you do your vocal tract. The machine is bound to move a bit more slowly than your tongue.

Still, mechanical speakers offer an interesting look at the way we speak. More so than the electronic synthesizers you'll read about in Chapter 3.

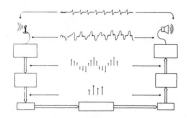

Chapter 3
Synthesizing Speech

The term synthesis implies the organized combination of separate or subordinate parts into a new form. In the case of speech synthesis, this refers to taking sounds and noise and combining them into words and phrases. Regardless of the specific technology or theoretical approach that a manufacturer takes, a device must, at some point, perform this basic function in order to synthesize speech.

Early mechanical speech synthesizers combined sounds in the same way that the human vocal tract does—controlling the placement of obstructions in an airflow and the resonances of the cavities in the air's path. This was fine as far as it went, but hard to use (not to mention impractical for mass marketing).

The advent of electronic computers, and especially microcomputers, opened new doors to engineers who would provide our machines with voices. Some hoped to better understand the way we speak; other designers labored to give increasingly intelligent machines an appropriately humanistic means of communication.

The compactness of microelectonic circuitry has allowed designers to place voice circuits in the smallest of appliances and toys. The question is no longer "can we give this a voice?" but rather, "what technology should we use to put the voice in?"

FROM VODERS TO PRERECORDED VOICES

An early attempt to produce speech, demonstrated at the 1939 and 1940 World Fairs, required a highly skilled operator. Termed the Voder, for "voice-operation demonstrator," the device comprised electrical networks which the operator selected with finger-operated keys. Ten keys operated potentiometers placed at the output of bandpass filters. These selected the resonance of the vocal tract. Three more keys selected additional filters that could be excited to produce stop consonant sounds. A wrist bar selected the noise source—the operator chose between a relaxation oscillator and a random noise source.

The Voder served as an electrically operated analog of the vocal tract. The resonant cavities had become filtered circuits. The articulator actions had become keyed circuit changes. Still, the operation was manual. Some of the cumbersome mechanical action of the earlier synthesizers was eliminated by electronics, but by no means all. The Voder's operator was still required to be a skilled instrumentalist.

1939 saw the introduction of the next great step toward electronic synthesis. The Voder evolved, becoming the Vocoder. Developed by Homer Dudley of Bell Labs, the Vocoder totally eliminated the operator as a performer. The Vocoder actually derived voice codes it could use at a later time to reproduce speech!

The Vocoder's input circuitry comprised a spectrum analyzer that could detect the presence of energy in 10 discrete frequency bands. These bands broke up the entire range of frequencies within which you could expect to hear any sounds that would have an impact on the pronunciation of a word—from 0 to 2950 Hz. An additional circuit on the Vocoder's input, called a frequency discriminator, determined the fundamental frequency of the incoming signal. This frequency gave a general idea of the pitch of the speech.

The 10 bandpass filters that the spectrum filter employed, and the frequency discriminator, operated in parellel. Thus, the Vocoder derived 11 bits of data about the incoming signal at the same time.

With an analysis technique for obtaining information about the nature of the speech signal, the groundwork was laid for today's digital computers to become involved in the process. What better tool for processing speech parameters than a computer? Although contemporary speech-analysis algorithms might be far more sophisticated than Dudley's, the theory is exactly the same. By capturing characteristics of the speech wave—acoustic parameters—you can recreate that wave at a later time.

The quality of today's analog-to-digital conversion equipment is high enough that it isn't necessary to look for speech parameters, however. If an analog-to-digital converter (ADC) samples the incoming signal at a high enough rate it can actually store a digital representation of the entire signal in memory. This is termed waveform encoding, and there are several methods of performing it—many of them good enough that you would find it difficult, if not impossible, to differentiate from the original speech.

Whether a synthesizer analyzes a signal and derives codes for reproducing the signal later, or simply converts the analog signal into its digital representation, the words thus encoded must be available to it for synthesis. To some extent, therefore, both parameter-encoding and waveform-encoding schemes bear a resemblance to analog tape recorders. They can't reproduce any sound or word that hasn't been encoded.

Some experts, such as Computalker Consultants' Ron Anderson, call these devices solid-state tape recorders. They fit only a restricted version of the definition of a synthesizer.

Even as a solid-state tape recorder, however, these devices represent a giant technological leap over either analog tape recorders or the optical disks that the telephone company (and other voice-response users) began using. These were the machines that told you the number you had called wasn't in service, that they weren't able to complete your call as dialed, or some other such message.

The optical disk suffered from a speech handicap that relates to the physics of its construction. Suppose you wanted to play back two words (messages, digits, or whatever) that were recorded sequentially on the disk. So long as you wanted to play them back in the same order that they were recorded in, you have no problem. If the circumstances dictate that the second message should be played first, however, you'd have to wait for a complete rotation of the disk. This is termed the system's latency time. In this particular case, we would say that the messages were located physically close, but were logically distant. Of course, one rotation of the disk doesn't take much time. But, if you had to piece together a long message from bits and pieces scattered about the disk's surface, the speech would begin to sound choppy. If the speech gets uneven enough, it can become difficult to understand.

Solid-state devices don't take any longer to play back any one utterance than another, regardless of where it's located. Thus, once you establish the speech rate (the timing of the utterances), the speech remains fairly constant.

The telephone companies now have begun to switch over to the solid-state device. Master Specialties provides an Audio Playback Unit (APU) Number Announcer (among many other voice-output products for this market) that announces the 10 numeric words "zero" through "nine." This device verifies subscriber lines. It accepts tone inputs and decodes them, while telling the operator what number was dialed. The block diagram shown in Fig. 3-1 illustrates how the device is configured.

THE SPEECH CHIPS

One of the first industrial-speech units came from Texas Instruments. Figure 3-2 gives you an idea of what the chip looks like with its epoxy off (and enlarged a few times). The company has gotten several patents for work that was necessary to make this chip function properly. Certain elements, such as the lattice filter, were considered innovative enough to be granted patents individually. The TMS5200 speech chip is intended to work with microcomputer systems. It's currently being used to give a voice to the firm's own TI-99/4 home-computer speech peripheral. Although the chip has its own 128-bit first-in, first-out (FIFO) buffer, it can also accept data directly from a TMS6100—a compatible 128k-bit read-only memory (ROM). By using the buffer, the host computer doesn't have to wait until the speech chip is done talking before doing some other task. It can load the buffer, turn on the speech chip, and then take care of other system tasks while the speech chip speaks the words in the buffer (about 50 milliseconds worth of speech).

Figure 3-3 illustrates TI's concept of solid-state speech. This model uses linear-predictive coding to encode the speech and then play it back later. Experts in physiology, applied mathematics,

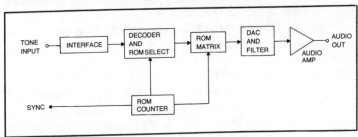

Fig. 3-1. The block diagram for a telephone annunciator.

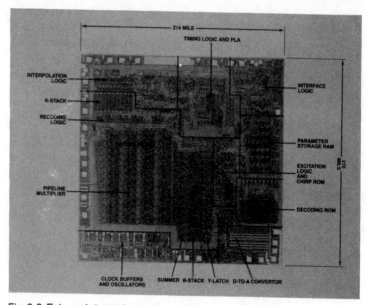

Fig. 3-2. Enlarged photo of a speech clip (courtesy of Texas Instruments Inc.).

acoustics, psychophysics, phychology, digital-signal processing and integrated circuit design all joined forces to create TI's particular version.

LPC comprises a technique of analyzing and synthesizing human speech by viewing the vocal tract as at time-varying filter. By exciting the filter with either random or periodic inputs, and reenacting the action of the filters over time, the chip speaks. An on-chip 8-bit digital-to-analog (D/A) converter transforms the filtered digital information into synthetic speech.

The chips aren't cheap yet—the TMS5200, in 100-piece quantities, costs $100 per chip. Yet, when you view the cost of previous talking machines, it seems dirt cheap. The fact that the entire speech unit comes in a single chip saves designers money. The space savings account for much.

Because TI's approach deliberately throws away some of the information contained in speech, the chip's speech doesn't sound quite human. Yet the savings of eliminating information that doesn't contribute to the intelligibility of the speech is enormous.

The parameters that tell the chip how to vary its 10-pole filter to emulate the vocal tract can't be generated by the chip. The process of converting speech into encoded parameters still takes a large computer and special algorithms. Thus, using the chip means

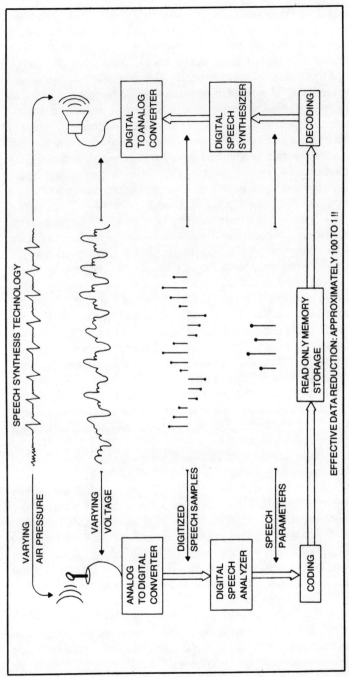

Fig. 3-3. Texas Instruments' view of solid-state speech.

using a ROMed word set (a vocabulary encoded in solid-state memory) that the manufacturer provides. You can order a custom vocabulary, but the encoding process is fairly expensive. The manufacturer must encode the words for you. When the speech chips first came out, vocabulary choices were few. In order to sell the devices, TI needed a way to allow large-quantity users to customize the vocabulary. The procedure that developed was for the user to figure out which words he needed for the application and then make a high-quality recording of those words being spoken. This let the user decide who would say the words and how they would be said. TI then encoded the words. A computer program converted the taped speech into the parameters that would cause the speech chip to say the words properly.

A company that used this encoding service was offered two possible prices. Encoding 10 to 24 words costs $225 per word. But, if the customer was willing to let Texas Instrument add the encoded word to its own library of words and phrases, the price dropped to $140 per word.

As a result, TI now has a library of encoded utterances representing a variety of applications and speakers. For the TMS5200, for example, the library contains 600 words spoken in a male voice and 50 in a female voice. If your application can use any of these canned words, you only have to pay $50 per word to have it put in your EPROM. Because the words are said by a variety of speakers, this approach might not suit your application. For games or toys or government projects, you might need words unique to your task. Yet, for a large number of users, the library represents a tremendous cost savings.

Getting started with TI's speech chips is also helped along by two speech-evaluation kits. The TMSK201 kit provides a TMS5200 speech chip and an EPROM containing 32 words, two phrases and one tone. Complete with all the documentation you'll need to get started using speech, the kit costs only $140.

Texas Instruments has another speech chip, and, of course, an evaluation kit to go along with it. The TMS 5100 chip is yours along with a ROM containing 204 words in the TNSK101 kit. This kit also comes with complete documentation and costs $140. Not bad pricing for a starter set.

In Fig. 3-4 you'll see one application of TI's speech chips. The TM990/306 speech board is designed to work easily with the line of microcomputer products that the firm sells to companies using processors for industrial purposes. The 306 board is designed for

Fig. 3-4. The Model 306 speech board (courtesy of Texas Instruments Inc.).

51

the industrial market. Its vocabulary, specialized to the task just as the hardware is, signals things that might come. Specialized hardware and software have already secured a place in the market. Data-acquisition systems are but one example. In the case of voice-output boards and peripherals, the software will include the word set. For, in the case of TI's chips at least, the encoded parameters are little more than microcode.

Another firm that produces chips which model the vocal tract and use firmware (software) to speak is General Instrument. Its SP-0250 and -0256 chips serve two distinctly different markets. The SP-0256 works as a standalone synthesizer. All you must do is add a few inexpensive components. This NMOS devices offers internal filters that model the vocal tract, a 16k ROM that stores the program and word data (parameters), a microcontroller that controls the flow of data from the ROM to the filter (the data flow actually determines the speech output) and a digital-to-analog converter that produces the final speech.

The SP-0250 is less capable on its own. It's designed to be part of a system. Yet, once put with other components, it provides a more versatile speech unit than the 256 can provide.

The block diagram shown in Fig. 3-5 gives you a look inside this 28-pin integrated circuit. To make it talk, you must add, as a minimum, a controller, such as General Instrument's PIC1650, a +5-volt power supply and a 3.12-MHz crystal oscillator.

General Instrument calls its speech products Orator. And to ensure that you have no trouble getting the chips orating, the firm even offers a single-board speech unit that puts the SP-0250 through its paces. The VSM-2032 comprises the 250 speech chip, 30 seconds of speech stored in ROM (32 words and syllables), 200 milliwatts of audio output power and a PIC1650 microcontroller on one 3.25 × 5 inch board. The $99 board gives you a single-board synthesizer at a very competitive price.

SPEAKING DIFFERENTLY

Of course both Texas Instruments and General Instrument use linear-predictive coding (LPC) to store and output speech. There are differences between the two (TI uses a 10-pole lattice filter and GI uses a 12-pole filter, to name but one), but the speech quality will be about the same. And this isn't the only way you can encode and play back human speech. So what other technologies are available?

In Japan the most popular method of modeling the vocal tract is called partial autocorrelation (PARCOR). This was originally developed by Nippon Telephone and Telegraph Corporation. Using this strategy, Matsushita Electric's MN6401, shown in Fig. 3-6, can synthesize as many as 63 words in either a male or female voice. A speech-rate control lets you use the same chip in applications requiring high quality speech that you use in those that require a large vocabulary. By manipulating the control line you can select either to output 10 seconds of high-quality speech or 30 seconds of the device's sloppiest verbiage. This serves you well if you manufacture a number of speech-output devices for a range of applications. You can use one speech chip and just select the appropriate vocabulary (in ROM) and select the speech rate accordingly.

In spite of the announcement of several chips that use PARCOR, the Japanese haven't made much of a dent in the speech marketplace yet. Although Nippon Electric Company, and others, are introducing new board-level products, most of the Japanese speech chips go into consumer products built in-house. These are

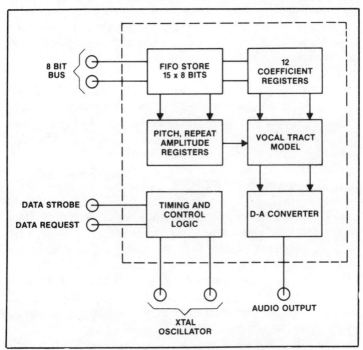

Fig. 3-5. General Instruments' SP-0250 provides versatile speech.

Fig. 3-6. A PARCOR speech chip—the MN6401 (courtesy of Matsushita Electric).

the chips that give voices to games, watches, and usually turn up in the talking appliances being rapidly introduced. It's easy to visualize a day, not too far away, when all clocks, televisions, microwaves and even doorbells will announce, rather than chime, click or ring.

As an example of the kinds of packaging that might envelope a specialized speech chip, consider the new talking voltmeter available from Franklin Institute Research Laboratory (Philadelphia, PA). The unit measures DC voltages from −40 to +40V with 0.1V resolution. Every seven seconds, or sooner if an operator commands it, the meter announces the displayed digits one at a time. In response to a 4.5V input, for example the meter says, "plus four point five."

This unit uses two microprocessors: one controls the system timing and input-signal processing, while the other selects the appropriate words (digits) from a speech ROM. The entire voltmeter weighs only 2.5 pounds and measures 2.5 × 10 × 9 inches and comes with its own 3-inch speaker and a NiCad (nickel-cadmium) battery pack. The speech circuitry doesn't result in a total package that's much different from comparable, but mute, meters from other manufacturers.

This is the trend you might expect to see. As speech technology moves into everyday devices, the only change will be the addition of a voice. Externally, these devices should remain the same. They'll do the same job and do it to the same degree and accuracy level as before. The method of implementing the voice—waveform encoding or parameter encoding—won't be an issue. Competition will center around the voice's quality and the appropriateness of its vocabulary to your particular needs.

Until recently, nearly all speech chips used some form of parameter encoding. Waveform encoding, even with compression techniques (strategies that use a computer to squeeze digital information so that it takes us less space), took far too much memory. Memory chips were expensive. Designers weren't interested in speech technology at the cost that these factors dictated.

National Semiconductor Corp. has broken new ground in waveform encoding, however. Working closely with experts at the University of California at Berkeley, they found a compression technique making waveform encoding a usable approach.

The chip samples at the same rate as previous chips—at least twice the highest frequency you are interested in synthesizing. This means the speech processor chip must operate at least 4k Hz. The new algorithm effectively reduces the amount of memory needed to store the information. Consider the job of storing the number 1000000, for example. In scientific notation, this number can be described as 10E6, ten to the sixth power. Storing 10E6 takes only four digits as opposed to the original seven. This oversimplifies what National Semiconductor has to do to reduce the storage requirements of words, of course.

The National Semiconductor speech synthesizer, just like the parameter encoded devices, requires a memory containing its vocabulary. This is usually a read-only memory that the manufacturer provides (in fact, with all of the chips discussed thus far you *must* buy the vocabulary from the manufacturer).

National has introduced a board that helps designers become familiar with its speech chips. This board, the DT1000 Digitalker (Fig. 3-7), provides everything that a designer needs to evaluate how well these chips will work in his design. The board comes with nearly everything you'd need to turn it on and listen to it talk. In fact, all you really need to add to do just that is a 9V power supply and a speaker. It already has a vocabulary of 138 words stored in two ROMs.

You can interface the Digitalker to your microprocessor system through its 22-pin edge connector. An on-board EPROM contains the software routines giving your system access to the speech functions of the board. This makes it simple to wire the board in and begin using it right away. The board's low cost ($495) makes it an ideal alternative to standalone synthesizers—especially when you intend to package the synthesizer inside the package of your product anyway.

National intends to make using speech technology even easier as time goes on. If you build a computer system with national's BLX piggyback connectors (or even the iSBX connectors from Intel), you'll be able to upgrade your computer system (add a voice to it) by plugging in one module. The first generation of such modules will come with 150 or so words in ROM. The actual vocabulary sizes available will depend in part on the voice quality National chooses to provide. Because of the nature of waveform encoding, the higher the voice quality, the more memory storing any given word takes.

The module approach lets you buy just the features you need. If you don't want a voice on your CPU board, you don't have to buy one. If you do, then you simply specify the voice module and plug it in. This will keep the costs of future microcomputer systems on a par with the performance they actually provide. You won't pay for features you don't want or need.

More boards will follow the introduction of the voice-synthesizer module, including a fully integrated board which will combine a complete processor system with the necessary voice components. Not everyone prefers modular construction, after all. Thus, you'll have a great deal of choice in designing voice into your products, not only about the particular chips you use, but about the way you use them. You can pick chip components that you build into your design (with a little help from the evaluation board); you can opt for plug-in modules; you can buy a board-level synthesizer that might provide its own intelligence for real-time operation. Why should the CPU get involved in the voice's activities?

You'll have more choice about the vocabulary that's available, too. National plans to introduce development software for its speech products to provide the same quality of support the firm provides for any other microcomputer product. Intended to run on the Starplex development system, the first software package will help you build custom vocabulary ROMs. National Semiconductor will bear the cost of encoding enough words (perhaps 10,000) that you'll be certain to find the exact words you need. This vocabulary superset will come on a floppy disk. You'll simply select the words

Fig. 3-7. The Digitalker speech board (courtesy of National Semiconductor).

on the disk that your application needs, link them together in a special file and execute a PROM-programming routine that will store those words in the memory. To add a bit of class, you'll even be able to choose whether you want a male or female speaker.

SPEECH WITHOUT RESTRICTION

For some manufacturers and some designers, any restriction on the speech a synthesizer can output is too much. These firms cannot accept the limitations of a pre-encoded vocabulary. They seek the ultimate in voice synthesis: unrestricted speech output.

Computalker Consultants used to manufacture a board that could produce unrestricted speech. Working from a computer program that parsed words and used rules to determine how to pronounce words, the board provided intelligible speech if you knew how to encode phonemes. This synthesis-by-rule approach proved popular, as did the fact that the board worked with the popular S-100 bus, and it attracted a following. The manufacturer was not happy, however. The voice quality was erratic and marginal. The company took its board off the market until these problems could be fixed. After considering to upgrade the board, Computalker finally shelved the project. "The state of the art isn't good enough," explained the firm's vice president, Ron Anderson.

Although Computalker Consultants still believes synthesis-by-rule is the one truly viable approach to board-level synthesizers, the firm considers today's components as marginal. They wait, and consult on, the next generation of speech chips.

The next generation of voice chips has already come. Already a leader in the business of building standalone synthesizers, Votrax introduced its SC-01. This single chip stores basic phonological speech sounds (phonemes) in ROM. You can combine these sounds to produce any word your application demands. No previous word encoding is necessary.

Storing phonemes rather than complete words not only removes any vocabulary limitations but also lets the system operate at lower data rates. Accurately reconstructing speech from digital data can require 2K bits per second or more; the SC-01 requires only 70 to 100 bits per second to output words.

You will need an algorithm (computer program) to decide what phonemes to select for a particular word, however (see Chapter 4), unless you want to spell every word out phonetically. It takes a 6-bit command to select any given phoneme. Each phoneme's duration is fixed: The slowest takes 250 milliseconds, while the fastest says its piece in 40 milliseconds. You have three pause phonemes to choose from to create the silence that should come between words or phrases. Two input bits set the average speech level and the chip takes care of varying the pitch to improve the intelligibility.

Votrax didn't find many takers for its CDS-1 developments system, which was designed to help designers write programs for the SC-01. In order to get people started, therefore, the firm developed an evaluation board. Like National's Digitalker, the board was intended to show users how to extend the limits of the chip (with a little careful design) and how to select the proper phonetic encoding for words they wanted to use.

The evaluator board comes with an SC-01 synthesizer chip, a 6808 microprocessor, both parallel and RS-232C (serial) interfaces, a RAM buffer in excess of 1K bytes long, a vocabulary in ROM containing 2000 words, an on-board audio amplifier and at least one empty memory socket. This socket is provided for you to add words to the board's vocabulary.

The word set contained in ROM provides two functions—you get a healthy-sized vocabulary allowing you to begin using the board immediately; you can learn from the phonetic codings how to properly encode the words you want to use.

Three basic operational modes let you use the words in the vocabulary, access the phonemes directly (just as if you had no stored words), or mix the two methods. Furthermore, you can affect the way the board speaks. This comes in handy if you want to generate sound effects. You have control over the master clock, and the master clock affects all speech parameters. Changing the clock speed while the board is talking can produce eerie effects. You can make the board speak rapidly, and in a high-pitched voice (the chipmunk voice) or drop its speech rate low to sound like a monster from the bogs. Some standard subroutines come with the board to get you started using this feature. After you understand how it acts, you can write your own specialized routines for the effects you want.

A variable-speech-rate option gives the board a feature not available with the chip alone. You can use external timing to change the speech rate without changing any other parameters. Thus, if you want the speech to be rapid, but otherwise normal, you can use this feature to great advantage.

Part of the point of this evaluation board is to act as a sort of hardware application note—living proof of the capabilities of the

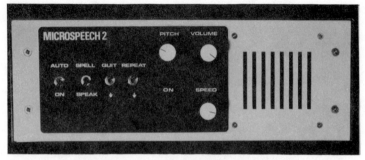

Fig. 3-8. The Microspeech2 (courtesy of Costronics Electronics).

SC-01. Its other quality is to work as a board-level synthesizer that a designer can build into his own product. Votrax intends the evaluation board as the first of a long product line to explore and exploit the virtues of phoneme synthesis.

SYNTHESIZERS BY THEMSELVES

You don't have to be a design engineer to have access to a synthesizer. Many units will plug into your computer to give it a voice. Unfortunately, the quality of that voice often depends on your ability to program the computer effectively, as you'll see in Chapter 4. The Microspeech2, shown in Fig. 3-8, comes in two models—one that accepts phonetic codes and one that will convert English text to phonemes and then output the word. Thus, you *can* sidestep the issue of learning to program the synthesizer yourself. Whether or not this solution will prove effective over the long run depends on your system and your needs.

Votrax, in addition to manufacturing speech chips and evaluation boards (and special-purpose synthesizers for the handicapped), also makes the synthesizers that work for several languages and synthesizers that suit business purposes. Each of these offers special features suitable for its particular market. The Multilingual ML-I (Fig. 3-9), for example, requires more phonemes than Votrax's other synthesizers. The synthesizer must be able to make all of the basic speech sounds for whatever language it will speak. In this case, each 12-bit command word that the host computer sends to the synthesizer selects the phoneme and speech characteristics. It takes seven bits to select one of the synthesizer's 122 phonemes; three bits select one of eight inflection (pitch) levels; two bits select one of four phoneme rates (duration). These versatile controls have allowed ML-I users to create vocabularies of over 300,000 words. Such flexibility isn't

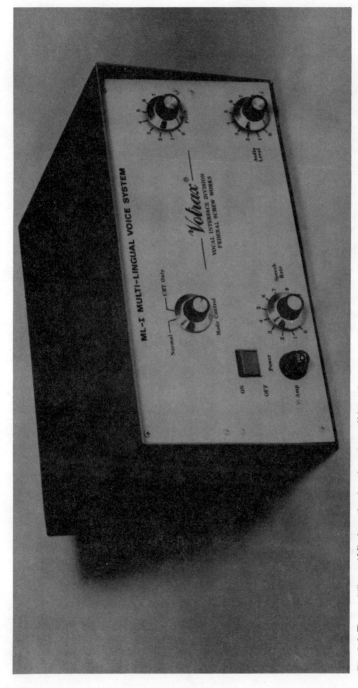

Fig. 3-9. The multilingual ML-1 synthesizer (courtesy of Votrax).

61

systems cost from $6710 to $7854, depending on the interface that your system requires.

The LVM-70 Business Communicator works in the business environment. It operates directly as an attached computer peripheral or as a remote data concentrator in a communications network. It can handle up to 64 telephone lines, accepting push-button telephone-tone inputs and providing a voice response. A unit that will accommodate four lines costs $8750; a 64-line unit costs $50,750.

In the area of low-cost synthesis, Votrax offers the Audio 1 for PET computers that need a voice. The $395 unit uses a proportional storage technique to reduce memory usage. Memory requirements must be held down for any synthesizer that will serve the hobby or personal computers. Whenever you classify a device as low-cost, the implication is that its low initial cost won't be offset by immense memory requirements.

Votrax has even made the Audio 1 useful to less experienced computer users. Instead of leaving you with a synthesizer for which you must write software, the firm has made life a little easier. You can use pushbuttons on the device to program it to output a 400-word to 500-word vocabulary.

Thus, you can see the differences among these synthesizers really have little to do with how they produce their sounds. It wouldn't matter to the ultimate user what technique the manufacturer used to get the messages out. The things that matter are the features that relate to the task; the conveniences that anticipate the needs of the user or designer. As more manufacturers introduce voice products, this is the form that the competition will take.

Phoneme isn't the only kind of synthesis you'll find used in standalone synthesizers. Take, for example, the VS10 synthesizer from Sun Electronics Corp. It uses LPC to provide a good voice quality from a pre-encoded vocabulary. Now, the only problem with a pre-encoded vocabulary is that the designer, at some point, must have a clear idea of what the synthesizer will have to say. Everything that it might need to say. Furthermore, you need to build quite a few units with the same vocabulary before you pay off the $2000 it costs to encode the words.

The VS10 synthesizer is actually two boards: the voice-data control board (Fig. 3-10) and the synthesizer board (Fig. 3-11). The control board relies on a Z80 microprocessor to control the synthesizer and the interface unit, as well as edit the voice data. It comes with 1K byte of ROM and 2K bytes of RAM. The ROM

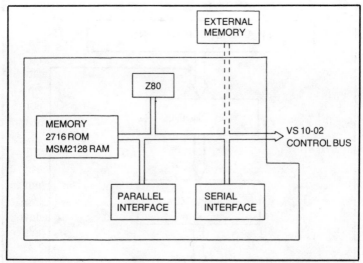

Fig. 3-10. The VS-10 synthesizer's voice-data control board (courtesy of Sun Electronics Corporation).

contains the software the controller needs to do its job. You can populate the board with up to 32K bytes of memory. If you store speech data in ROM and store it here, you have access to a large

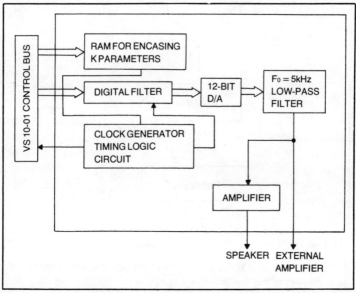

Fig. 3-11. The VS-10 synthesizer board's block diagram (courtesy of Sun Electronics Corporation).

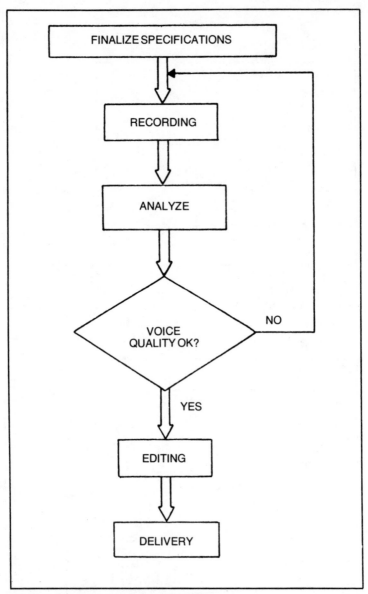

Fig. 3-12. The custom word-encoding process.

fixed vocabulary. If you have the unit connected to a host computer, you can populate the memory space with RAMs and download voice data to the RAMs from the host computer, providing an even larger vocabulary.

The VS10-02 synthesizer board comprises a digital filter, a 12-bit D/A converter, a low-pass filter that eliminated sounds above 5 kHz and 1.5-watt audio amplifier.

Because the synthesizer does use parameter encoding (LPC), you must have the manufacturer encode the words for you. The process of custom encoding words follows the flowchart shown in Fig. 3-12. Together with the manufacturer you establish a word list. You can prepare an open-reel tape recording of someone saying the words, or Sun Electronics can have it done for you (for an additional fee, of course). Sun analyzes the spoken words and produces the parameter analysis the firm thinks will cause the synthesizer to output exactly what you want. Using a synthesizer

Fig. 3-13. Sperry Univac's Voice Response Unit (VRU) suits sophisticated applications such as air control.

65

and the parameters, the manufacturer prepares an audition tape. If it sounds good to you, it goes into ROM. After you've paid the one-time $2000 encoding fee, VS10's will cost you $1500 each (10) or $1000 (100).

The VS10 typifies the class of boxed synthesizers that will be sold to original equipment manufacturers (OEM) who don't want to repackage the synthesizer. The value they will add to the product will come in the form of software and hardware that makes the synthesizer useful to you. Alternatively, the designer can use the synthesizer to make his system useful to you.

You'll find synthesizers cropping up all over. Sperry Univac makes a voice-response system (Fig. 3-13) that, although you'll never see it in your neighborhood store, might affect your life dramatically. The VRU-401 voice-response unit has found acceptance in applications such as air control. The voice which tells the pilot of the jumbo jet you're riding in where he is, might come from such a unit.

Naturally, these large-scale units take advantage of the same technologies that are making the personal-computer voices viable. Solid-state memories let the system patch together phrases from prerecorded vocabularies without losing intelligibility. Microprocessor control lets designers implement more sophisticated control algorithms. The problem that these two technologies must tackle, the weak link in pre-recorded voice-response technology, comes in between pre-recorded utterances. If you listen closely to the new systems (and not so closely to older systems) you can hear the concatenation effect. The utterances aren't said in a way that makes them sound right when they're butted up against another phrase.

A technique called adaptive differential pulse code modulation (ADPCM) has reduced the memory needed to encode any particular utterance by half. Furthermore, multiplexing audio lines allows common system elements to be shared among several users. These strategies have made high-quality voice-response systems cost effective for many applications. The block diagram in Fig. 3-14 illustrates how this works. Although multiple users can access the system through the various audio channels, the only hardware that must be duplicated is that directly involved in making an audio channel available. Everything else is shared throughout the system.

As more systems become available, they will find use in more applications. As the systems find their way into new applications,

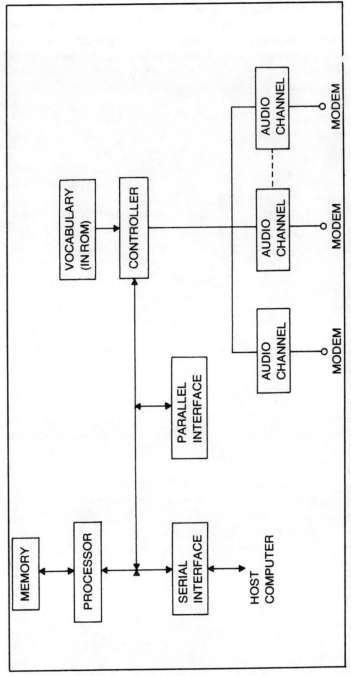

Fig. 3-14. Differential pulse-code modulation reduces the memory requirements for each utterance.

67

manufacturers will gain a better understanding of what their customers need and how to provide it. The future of voice synthesis, however, rests largely on the shoulders of the semiconductor manufacturers. And some of them have surprises in store for all of us.

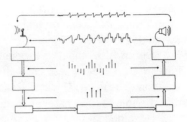

Chapter 4

Converting Text To Speech

If you add speech to your computer by buying one of the devices which has a set of vocabulary words stored in ROM, using the voice will be quite simple. All the computer needs to do is determine which word or words it wants spoken and then tell the synthesizer to output that word. Typically the software handles this task. A routine will look up the address where the word is stored and pass that value to the synthesizer. It's not always a trivial programming task, but it won't get out of hand either.

But what if you have one of those synthesizers without a fixed vocabulary? Now the task gets a bit more difficult. You'll have to develop software that not only addresses the speech sounds stored in the synthesizer, but that can establish accurately which sounds are needed to output a certain word.

MATCH THE SYNTHESIZER TO THE APPLICATION

You can know in advance what words a synthesizer will have to say. Some applications don't require a large vocabulary at all. A talking multimeter, for example, only has to be able to report on a voltage; restricting its vocabulary to words associated with that job doesn't seem unreasonable at all.

In many applications, in fact, a versatile speech-output system could provide more confusion than clarity. A computer's message should be clear, intelligible, concise and relevant. For most applications you won't want the machine to wax poetic.

There are applications which won't tolerate a limited vocabulary at all, however. In these you might not be able to determine ahead of time what words will be needed. You might wish to have a synthesizer on hand for use in a variety of applications. In an engineering lab a dedicated synthesizer would have limited application, whereas one that can speak any words needed would suit nearly any job.

Kurzweil Computer Products found one application where unrestricted speech was not only the best solution, but the only solution. The firm's Desktop Reading Machine, shown in Fig. 4-1, must be able to say whatever happens to be in a text placed upon it.

Designed to free the blind from reliance on Braille translations of books and magazines, and any other printed matter, the reading machine reads aloud. You simply place the text face down on the reading machine to hear it. Cameras scan the page, identifying letters, letter groups and symbols. This process results in an ASCII representation of the word, the same thing you'd get by typing the words into a computer through a keyboard. Then comes the crucial step. The machine converts the English text into speech.

The task of speaking in the Kurzweil machine falls to an unrestricted speech synthesizer. Even if the manufacturer could find an economical means of storing enough words in memory to accommodate every possible text, the job of looking up each word's memory location would prove unmanageable. The reading process would wallow along. Part of the reading machine's success, in fact, has come from its ability to read at a conversational pace with good stress and intonation—factors that contribute to a high level of intelligibility.

Unhappy with the performance level of the unrestricted-speech synthesizers available at the time, Kurzweil developed its own unit. Yet, the task the software must perform remains the same. The words read in the text must be converted to sounds before they can be synthesized!

STORE SOUNDS, NOT WORDS

The basic argument for unrestricted speech output revolves around two factors: the large number of vocabulary items you'd need to handle most English text, and the quality of the output when words are concatenated into sentences.

According to Hugo Feugen, General Health Corporation's vice president for computer development, a vocabulary large enough to speak a variety of English-language texts equally well could require up to 50,000 words in memory. But Feugen is more concerned about the second problem. "Concatenated speech (words strung one after another) is very difficult to understand, especially for long utterances," he says. "Intonation is missing. Proper stresses are missing. Syllable timing will be incorrect."

The problem with concatenating words is that we don't always say a word just one way. When the manufacturer encodes a word, it strives to make the word as clear and intelligible as possible when it's spoken. When you put two words together, however, pronunciation changes. You might drop the ending of one word simply because of the beginning of the next word. If you don't understand how this causes problems, go back and read the section on coarticulation in Chapter 2.

Obviously, then, storing words in memory and playing them back won't provide satisfactory sentences no matter how hard we try to encode them properly. You can't know how to encode them until you know the context they'll be spoken in.

So how do we get unrestricted speech? We turn, as Kurzweil did, to synthesis techniques that let us combine speech sounds to create the word and pronunciation needed at each moment. The first unrestricted-speech synthesizers all used phoneme synthesis. It is still the most common approach. We covered much of the basic information about phoneme synthesis in our discussion of the devices themselves in Chapter 3, but now we have to put the technology to work.

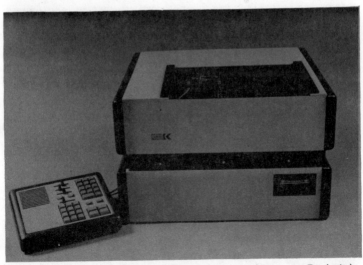

Fig. 4-1. Desktop Reading Machine (courtesy of Kurzweil Computer Products.).

The synthesizer's basic operation is simple. You provide a phoneme synthesizer with the code for a phoneme and it says that sound. You string several phonemes together, along with the appropriate pitch and intonation information, and the synthesizer says a word.

That's the easy part. More difficult is the process of determining which phonemes you'll need. How do you select from the innumerable combinations that you might make out of 100 or so phonemes?

PROGRAMMING PRODUCES PHONEMES

The task of providing instructions to a phoneme synthesizer usually falls to the host computer. An algorithm will take the text, encoded in ASCII characters, and convert the words into phoneme codes and speech parameters. The flowchart shown in Fig. 4-2 illustrates one approach to this problem. This program uses several levels of analysis to derive enough information to speak the words clearly. The step labeled "IDENTIFY FEATURE ENVIRONMENTS" is particularly important. It's at this point the program looks at the context in which the word is spoken. We'll see what the program does with that information shortly.

Doing a good job of converting words into sound codes that will make a synthesizer speak properly requires a strong understanding of linguistics—the science of languages. Anyone who has tried to learn a new language has encountered the problem of attempting to read, and pronounce correctly, words written in a language they don't yet understand. There are many subtle factors entering into pronunciation, factors difficult to put into a set of rules. The pronunciation rules in English sometimes seem to have more exceptions than normal cases. This same problem faces the programmer using a synthesizer for voice output. What is needed is a set of rules simple enough to work quickly and yet comprehensive enough to handle most of the common but subtle pronunciation problems.

The requirement for the rules to be simple comes from the application. The more complex you make the rules, the longer it will take to figure out the appropriate phonemes. Part of the effectiveness of voice output is its immediacy. You don't want to throw away this major benefit to improve pronunciation just a little bit more. You'll have to find the correct compromise position by trial and error. There's no easy test for either complexity or pronunciation. Undoubtedly you'll need to have potential users

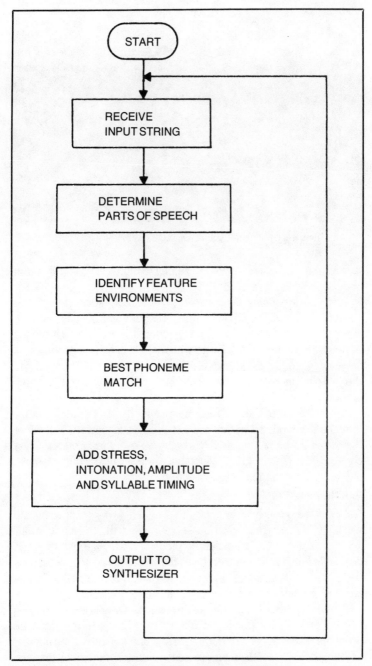

Fig. 4-2. A flowchart for a text-to-English conversion program.

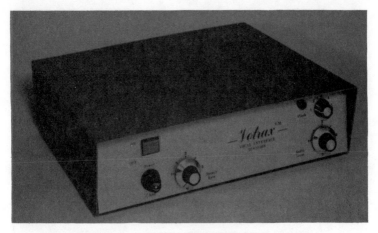

Fig. 4-3. The VS-6.0 phoneme synthesizer (courtesy of Votrax).

listen to the voice of the system and have them tell you if they can understand what it says.

If you are using a phoneme synthesizer, such as Votrax's VS-6.0 (Fig. 4-3), you'll be trying to output a set of codes such as those shown in Table 4-1. The 63 phonemes cover enough sounds to produce English words quite well and German and Spanish to a lesser degree. There are several programs available that perform the text-to-phoneme conversion, and we'll examine their key points.

It's easiest to think of the software in terms of other software that is more familiar. In this case, it seems appropriate to think of the program as a two-pass compiler. First the program must convert ASCII text into phonemes; then it must convert these phonemes into machine-readable codes.

PARSING A WORD

To see exactly how such an English-text compiler would work, let's convert a word ourselves. We will, to maintain our analogy, hand compile a selected piece of text. Suppose that it is desirable for the synthesizer to say the word "sort." In its first pass the compiler determines that these letters, linked together in this particular manner would be pronounced "s ow r t." This is the ARPABET phonetic spelling of the word. The phonetic spelling serves only one purpose: it shows how each letter must be pronounced in the context of the word. Unfortunately, the phonetic spelling doesn't make any more sense to the synthesizer than the original text did.

To take the word one step closer to machine language, let's convert the ARPABET spelling to a phonetic spelling using the Votrax phoneme codes. This way the spelling will at least be in terms of the 63 sounds the synthesizer can produce. The Votrax spelling for "sort" is: 2/PA1, 2/S, 1/O, 1/R, 1/T. To translate back into English, the synthesizer will output two pauses, followed by two "S" phonemes, then one "O", one "R" and one "T."

Table 4-1 shows you the ASCII equivalents for these codes. Now that you know the appropriate sequence to get the word, you could simply send ASCII characters NC, NC, OA, FB, KB, JB to the synthesizer over a serial interface.

Suppose, however, that when you type the word in, the synthesizer's pronunciation doesn't sound quite right to you. The easiest way to fix the problem is to go straight to the intermediate code—the phonetic spelling—and change a few sounds. You could easily broaden the o in "sort," for example, by adding an extra vowel phoneme. If a double "O" sounds too thin, try following "O"

Table 4-1. Phoneme Synthesizers Operate From Phonetic Codes (courtesy of Votrax).

PHONEME	HEX	OCTAL	ASCII	PHONEME	HEX	OCTAL	ASCII
PA0	03	003	'C@'	EH1	02	002	'B@'
PA1	3E	076	'NC'	EH2	01	001	'A@'
A	20	040	'@B'	EH3	00	000	'@@'
A1	06	006	'F@'	ER	3A	072	'JC'
A2	05	005	'E@'	F	1D	035	'MA'
AE	2E	056	'NB'	G	1C	034	'LA'
AE1	2F	057	'OB'	H	1B	033	'KA'
AH	24	044	'DB'	I	27	047	'GB'
AH1	15	025	'EA'	I1	0B	013	'K@'
AH2	08	010	'H@'	I2	0A	012	'J@'
AW	3D	075	'MC'	I3	09	011	'I@'
AW1	13	023	'CA'	IU	36	066	'FC'
AW2	30	060	'@C'	J	1A	032	'JA'
AY	21	041	'AB'	K	19	031	'IA'
B	0E	016	'N@'	L	18	030	'HA'
CH	10	020	'@A'	M	0C	014	'L@'
D	1E	036	'NA'	N	0D	015	'M@'
DT	04	004	'D@'	NG	14	024	'DA'
E	2C	054	'LB'	O	26	046	'FB'
E1	3C	074	'LC'	O1	35	065	'EC'
EH	3B	073	'KC'	O2	34	064	'DC'
OO	17	027	'GA'	UH	33	063	'CC'
OO1	16	026	'FA'	UH1	32	062	'BC'
P	25	045	'EB'	UH2	31	061	'AC'
R	2B	053	'KB'	UH3	23	043	'CB'
S	1F	037	'OA'	V	0F	017	'O@'
SH	11	021	'AA'	W	2D	055	'MB'
T	2A	052	'JB'	Y	29	051	'IB'
TH	39	071	'IC'	Y1	22	042	'BB'
THV	38	070	'HC'	Z	12	022	'BA'
U	28	050	'HB'	ZH	07	007	'G@'
U1	37	067	'GC'	*NULL CODE	FF	377	'OO'

with an "AH." The phonetic spelling would now be 2/PA1, 2/S, 1/O, 1/AH, 1/R, 1/T.

The fact that you can make these adaptations will help make the speech smoother and more natural sounding. Some fine tuning must be left to the ear. If you find that a large number of words need the same fix, however, there's probably something wrong with the portion of the program that converts the text to phonemes. By changing the way it looks at combinations of phonemes you should be able to modify the rule that's causing the problem. Again, this takes time and patience. You are treading relatively new ground and much of the work is trial and error.

ESTABLISHING THE RULES

The step-by-step conversion of one word probably made the conversion process seem awfully simple. Well, it isn't. This particular example was simple. The word doesn't have any ambiguities in it. Each of its letters (called *orthographic* characters in the language of linguistics) relates or corresponds to one, and only one, phonetic symbol. Furthermore, the word has simple timing and stress, and takes only one syllable.

In most cases you won't be so lucky. In English the letter "e," for example, can be pronounced either long or short, and sometimes isn't pronounced at all. When it isn't pronounced, however, it tends to be more of a problem than when it is, for then it changes the way you say other letters in the word.

Take a look at the word "one." You don't say the "e" at all. But its presence causes you to say "one" differently than you say "on." When the computer program parses the word, therefore, it can't make decisions about how to pronounce the "o" until it knows that the last letter of the word is an "e." When it gets to the "e" it must not only backtrack to add information to its file on the "o" but must also understand that the "e" will be silent. This is not a pause, either: it is *silence*. Silence doesn't necessarily occupy time; a pause does. Your software will have to understand the difference if the speech is to sound natural.

This phenomenom of one phoneme affecting another characterizes speech. Linguists call it *phoneme interaction*. One important job the program has is deciding how far to extend the boundaries of interaction. Do the letters of one word affect adjacent words? You bet. But not with any sort of marked regularity. The first time you hear concatenated speech that doesn't take interword effects into account, it'll strike you as being—well—machine like.

Making speech isn't too bad a job. Making that speech sound natural can be complex.

Unhappily, many of the phoneme interactions, especially between words, aren't very well understood. That makes it hard to formulate rules. Another problem is the large number of exceptions there will be to any set of rules you can develop.

One approach that sounds good on paper is to identify words containing these exceptions and then store their pronunciations in memory. When the computer spotted one of these words in a sentence, rather than parse it, the program would simply look up the predetermined phonetic code for that word. The predetermined code would, of course, be determined by ear—trial and error. Unfortunately, English is a language of many exceptions. A dictionary or lookup table large enough to cover even the most commonly encountered words would be huge. You wouldn't save much over a system with all its vocabulary encoded. And there would still be words that you hadn't put in the dictionary that didn't fit the rules. You can't evaluate every combination of words and letters in advance.

MIX THE STRATEGIES

Well, if you can't store all of the difficult words in memory, and pronouncing all the words based on pronunciation rules causes problems, what's left? What you can do is find a balance between the two approaches.

At Bell Telephone Laboratory's Computer Science Center, an associative learning process uses pronunciation rules designed to handle both words and word fragments. Written by Bell's M. Douglas McIlroy, the program contains 750 pronunciation rules, plus a dictionary comprising 100 complete words, 580 word fragments and 70 individual letters.

It is the use of word fragments that effectively reduces the size of the dictionary. Many hard-to-pronounce words might all suffer from problems with the same word fragment. By isolating pronunciation problems into word fragments, McIlroy's program uses one dictionary entry to serve as several complete words. Where the problems are unique, the program stores a handmade pronunciation guide away for reference.

The program takes a great deal of memory. One version occupies 11K bytes in a PDP-11/45 minicomputer. Although you could run an 11K byte program on a microcomputer, it is too large for most practical applications. The program suffers from a few pronunciation deficiencies, too. McIlroy chose to ignore the effects that pitch and stress have on the way we say words. His efforts concentrated on other elements of intelligibility. You'll notice the absence of pitch and stress factors in the quality of the speech, however, and nearly everything that contributes to speech quality has a role in intelligibility. Adding these two simple factors to McIlroy's program would prove a monumental task. You'd quickly discover that stress and pitch are not trivial items to determine accurately.

UNCOVERING WORD STRUCTURES

Researchers at the Massachusetts Institute of Technology have taken the somewhat different tack of using the computer program to find linguistic structures. It turns out that if you reduce all phoneme combinations to structural features, or *morphological features* (to use the correct linguistic terminology), you can accomplish the same job as storing all phonetic spellings—and in far less space. Think of the analysis this way: Why store the phonetic codes for the ending "ing" for every word that needs it. when you can store the ending once?

So what the program does is examine each word carefully. It takes note of isolated roots and prefixes, contractions and suffixes. All of this information becomes grist for the pronunciation mill.

The designers of the program also added information about the way we actually read prose. This extra information allows the program to make intelligent decisions about where to place the stress, how vowels are reduced and the type of intonation that makes sense in a particular context. As a result, the program produces speech that sounds more like a human's and less like that of a machine enforcing a rigid set of pronunciation rules.

So the program at MIT pays attention to word structure, not just the letters that make it up. It combines a knowledge of word structures with practical speech studies to capture the flavor of our verbal style. The output is intelligible. Unfortunately, this program doesn't comprise a viable solution to unrestricted speech output either. Why doesn't it? The morphological table that forms the reference dictionary of the program contains 12,000 feature entries. The routines that store and use the prose-reading information add bulk to the program. The program quickly becomes behemoth, requiring a large-scale host computer with memory to spare. All this is for voice output? It isn't worth it.

SPEEDING UP THINGS

Using a program to search a morphological-feature table and then applying extra prose-reading rules to the output takes a great deal of time—too much, in fact. At the University of Illinois' Computer-Based Education Research Laboratory (CERL), researchers have successfully used a variation on MIT's technique. This strategy assumes that you can, with a reasonable amount of accuracy and consistency, associate a set of underlying properties (or features) with every orthographic character (letter). This means that each letter in our alphabet has certain characteristics. Although these characteristics might change slightly, depending on the morphological context the letter is placed in, the basic characteristics are still present in some form.

The exciting thing about this concept is that it allows you to replace the MIT dictionary and its 12,000 items with a lookup table that has only 26 entries—one for each letter. Obviously this 26-element table, or dictionary, will not cause the problems encountered in trying to use MIT's unwieldy one.

Each dictionary entry should be as small as possible if we want the program to run quickly. Yet, it's important to put as much information as possible about the letter's characteristics in the dictionary.

At General Health Corporation, Hugo Feugen has produced a compromise that suits a microcomputer system's requirements perfectly. His dictionary entries look like menus. An entry comprises a string of bits. One bit position represents a particular characteristic. If the feature is present in the letter the bit gets set to a ONE. If the feature isn't present, the bit stays ZERO. The dictionary entry can therefore hold enough information to tell us that a letter is:

☐ Fricative—a sound made by a disturbance of the air flow

☐ Lateral—a sound made by air escaping from the mouth laterally

☐ Resonant—a voiced-speech sound that uses one or more of the vocal tract's resonant cavities (such as the nasal cavity)

☐ Nasal—a quality added to speech by its passage through the nasal cavity

☐ Continuant—sustained or continued sound over a period of time.

The actual list of characteristics depends on the program's design. For each characteristic you must allocate another bit in each entry. That's 26 bits. Feugen's feature lists comprise 54 elements. Figure 4-4 illustrates the entry for the letter "B." The YES in front of features 5, 8, 30, 31 and 40 indicates that these are the characteristics of the letter. In the memory of the computer, the bits associated with these features will be set to ONE. The letter is consonant, obstruent, a stop, plosive and voiced.

The program parses a word and replaces each letter with a data structure that is really nothing more than a copy of the dictionary entry. So you now have a string of 54-bit data structures. The program can examine the pronunciation environment to uncover phonemic interaction. The software uses a set of rules governing *intermorphemic phenomena*. (This is another name for phonemic interaction that describes what is happening a bit more accurately. We have to appease the linguists.)

Suppose, for example, that one rule states:

A sibilant becomes palatized preceding palatial glides!

To the program this means that it must locate palatial glides and check the preceding letter to see if its sibilant bit (bit 9) is set. If it is, then the program modifies that letter's feature table by setting the palatal bit (bit 49).

Once the routine has satisfied the complete rule set, the feature table should represent the sound you want the synthesizer to output in the present context. The synthesizer has only 63 phonemes that it can produce, so something has to give.

The last task the software must deal with, therefore, is making a best-fit comparison. You want the program to select the sound (phoneme) that most closely matches the feature-table selection. The best phoneme might not be the obvious one. It depends on how many of the rules affected the utterance.

If the speech sounds odd, get a linguist to spell some words for you phonetically. Then compare those spellings to the phonemes the program chooses. Type the phonemes the linguist has provided into the synthesizer to ensure his spelling actually produces a more accurate (natural sounding) pronunciation than the one the program offered.

To learn the rules you'll have to consult several linguistics texts. In these you might find the pronunciation examples you need to give your system a thorough test. Lloyd Rice at Computalker Consultants likes to use a stanza or two from Edgar Allen Poe's *The Raven*.

The feature-table approach does two very nice things: It reduces the size of the dictionary, thereby speeding dictionary

#	Feature		#	Feature		#	Feature	
0	VOWEL		20	BACK		40	VOICED	
1	SPREAD		21	TENSE		41	DEVOICED	
2	ROUNDED		22	LAX		42	ASPIRATED	
3	COMPLEX		23	NASALIZED		43	SYLLABIC	
4	CONSONANT	YES	24			44	BILABIAL	YES
5	SEMI-VOWEL		25	PRIMARY		45	LABIO-DENTAL	
6	CONTINUANT		26	SECONDARY		46	DENTAL	
7	OBSTRUENT	YES	27	TERTIARY		47	ALVEOLAR	
8	SIBILANT		28	LONG		48	ALVEO-PALATAL	
9	LATERAL		29	SHORT		49	PALATAL	
10	RESONANT		30	STOP	YES	50	VELAR	
11	SONORANT		31	PLOSIVE	YES	51	UVULAR	
12			32	AFFRICATE		52	GLOTTAL	
13			33	FRICATIVE		53	GROOVED	
14			34	TRILL		54	BACK/VELAR	
15	HIGH		35	GLIDE				
16	MID		36	NASAL				
17	LOW		37	LENIS				
18	FRONT		38	FORTIS				
19	CENTRAL		39	MORAFIED				

SOUND #: 1   'B'
CHARACTERISTIC #:

Fig. 4-4. A derived feature table (courtesy of General Health Corporation).

searches and saving memory, and makes it a simple matter (relatively) to apply speech rules before saying the words. The program works well enough that it causes a Votrax VS-6.0 synthesizer to speak more naturally than when you use the phonetic codes for the words the manufacturer provides in the user's manual.

But the program does represent a compromise, both in terms of speech quality and operating speed. Yet, General Health's system does offer a viable combination of hardware and software for adding voice to a microcomputer system.

BUYING A SYSTEM OFF THE SHELF

Not everyone has the skills, desire or time to develop a suitable computer program for the sole purpose of making a machine talk. If you are designing a system that will incorporate a synthesizer chip, often your time is barely adequate for completing the system-design task without having to invent a technique for making the output device work.

In these cases, what you might be looking for is a system that would allow you to build a customized vocabulary and store it in ROM right in your own shop. What you need is a voice-oriented development system that will give you the same support for your voice chip which you needed for the microprocessor. Ideally, the development system should accept English text and output the codes needed to make the synthesizer speak properly.

Votrax's Customer Development System (CDS) does this quite nicely for its speech chip. The system (Fig. 4-5) even provides an *emulator* that lets you preview the speech. You type in the words and then listen to the emulator say them. If they don't sound quite right, you can fine tune the codes (in the same way we did in our hand compilation) to obtain a sweet-sounding system.

A system such as the CDS has one problem. You would have to be using an awful lot of Votrax's SC-01 synthesizer chips (Fig. 4-6) to justify the cost of a development system that does nothing but develop a custom vocabulary. The price is too high unless you are in the business of manufacturing a large number of speaking devices, each with a unique vocabulary.

Another development system will soon be equipment to do some vocabulary customization. If you want to use National Semiconductor's speech chip (or speech boards), you'll soon be able to use existing Starplex development systems to take words off of floppy disks, which National Semiconductor will provide, and

Fig. 4-5. The Customer Development System (CDS) (courtesy of Votrax).

put your word choices into ROM for the speech chip. You'll still be dependent on the manufacturer to encode the word for you, but National Semiconductor's commitment is to provide enough words on disk so this won't be a problem at all. The firm promises all the words that are fit to say.

UNRESTRICTED SPEECH FROM LPC CHIPS

Thus far, all the talk about unrestricted speech has revolved around phoneme synthesis. But, just when it began to look as if LPC synthesizer chips had hit their peak, that they weren't suited to applications requiring more freedom of speech, the manufacturers pull a surprise out of the technological hat.

Guess what? It's just as easy to put sounds into ROMs for LPC synthesizers as it is to fill them with words. Then, if you can write a software program that will convert English text into speech sounds . . . Begins to sound familiar, right? And it turns out that the reason we didn't hear about this sooner is that the LPC chip manufacturers were busily readying their text-to-speech software to sell along with the ROM containing speech sounds.

The sounds Texas Instruments stores in ROM are not phonemes, however. They are sounds representing the way phonemes sound after they've been modified. Thus, instead of converting a letter to a phoneme and then modifying the phoneme selection to reflect the pronunciation environment, these programs convert the letter to the correct sound, based on its environment.

The modified phonemes are called *allophones*, and stringing allophones together, provided you've made a careful selection of the proper sound, produces much more natural sounding speech than does concatenating phonemes. This results from the fact that you have more sounds to choose from. While a typical phoneme synthesizer offers 63 phonemes, Texas Instruments' allophone ROM gives you a choice of 128 allophones. After all, each time you modify a phoneme you produce an allophone. Thus, a program that operates exactly the way Hugo Feugen's does would be matched against many more (65 more) possible sounds when used with an allophone synthesizer than with the phoneme unit for which it was developed. The same program would therefore sound better.

The allophones that were encoded by Texas Instruments last from 50 to 250 milliseconds each. The entire 128-allophone library requires 3K bytes of memory.

Fig. 4-6. The first phonetic synthesizer on a chip—the SC-01 (courtesy of Votrax).

The firm provides a 7K-byte lookup table that converts text to allophones. Designed to work with its own TMS 5200 speech chip, the lookup table and allophone ROM adapt the LPC synthesizer for any application requiring unrestricted speech. Naturally you could still use complete words in ROM, too. With a little extra software, a system could identify words in its vocabulary and draw them directly from ROM while converting the rest of the text to allophones. This would serve to increase intelligibility by letting you store hard-to-pronounce words in their entirety.

Another firm has entered the unrestricted-speech market using LPC. Telesensory Systems has developed a proprietary digital speech-processor chip that suits LPC speech output. Like Texas Instruments, the firm has developed a set of allophones residing in ROM. The firm plans to introduce a complete board providing the speech chip, allophone library (in ROM) and a text-to-speech conversion program (also in ROM).

The growing number of commercially available text-to-speech programs, and their increasingly smaller size, means that single-board synthesizers which can produce natural-sounding unrestricted speech from printed text aren't far off. The lid is off the technology pot.

It might become difficult over time to find out exactly the technology being used to produce the speech. New devices, such

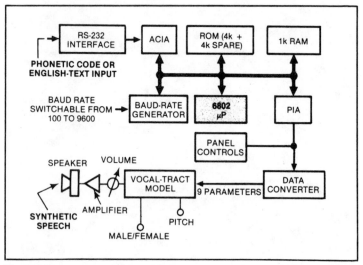

Fig. 4-7. The block diagram for Microspeech2 (courtesy of Costronics Electronics).

as signal-processor chips, can switch from LPC to formant synthesis at the flip of an instruction. As the allophone sets become richer and more mature, the speech will sound more natural, regardless of the chip techology you use. And the synthesizer that produces concatenated phonemes today could easily be modified to output allophones tomorrow.

At least one of the standalone phonemic synthesizers already comes with an optional text-to-speech conversion program. Costronics Electronics' Microspeech connects to a host computer over an RS-232 interface. The block diagram of the unit is shown in Fig. 4-7. Without the optional conversion routine, the synthesizer accepts phonetic codes that prove similar to the Votrax set shown in Table 4-1. This version costs about $2190. If you add the software, you can send ASCII characters straight to the synthesizer. With the optional software, the synthesizer goes for about $2375.

None of the synthesizers producing unrestricted speech will ever be confused with a human, except perhaps over a telephone line, but the speech sounds more natural every day. This field demands extensive research to identify the missing elements that make it difficult to take the final steps for intelligible and natural-sounding speech to human like speech.

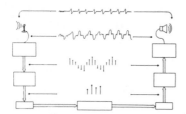

Chapter 5
First, Speech Recognition

Speech-recognition technology allows you to communicate with a computer or electronic system using the means that comes most naturally to you—your voice. Equipment that can use voice input to provide the operator's control can save both time and money, in spite of the fact that voice-recognition equipment capable of standing up to commercial applications still costs a pretty penny.

One of the foremost experts in the voice-recognition field, Dr. Wayne Lea, has reported on studies comparing typing skills to speaking skills. Typical speech, according to these studies, flows at a rate of 2 to 3.6 words every second. If you're an average unskilled typist, on the other hand, you get from 0.2 to 0.4 words on paper each second. And rushing out to take a typing class won't close the gap completely, either. A skilled typist only puts out from 1.6 to 2.5 words each second.

Even more important than speed, however, is accuracy. You don't make the kinds of mistakes when you speak which inevitably creep into typing—typographical errors. If you do make a mistake when entering data verbally, you would also make the mistake typing. It is an error of fact, not an entry error.

In the world of computers, each method of entering information into the computer is called an input modality. A modality, after all, is just a word that refers to a way of doing things. Anything. So the jargon "input modality" simply means a way of putting things in.

For a system designed to accept them all, voice, keyboards, switches, sensor transducers and light pens comprise examples of input modalities. Each of these techniques offers advantages for particular applications. If you are working on an electronic circuit, and the circuit's board layout has been stored in the computer, for example, the fastest method of indicating a particular component might be with a light pen. You touch the pen to the location of the component on a drawing of the circuit board that is shown on the screen of the computer.

Such an approach is effective because it provides a high density of information. When you touch the light pen to the location (one input), the system knows you are indicating the component's location in a two-dimensional grid. It stores the coordinates in memory. The single touch provides two input values. If you used a keyboard for entering the same data, you would have to use several keystrokes. As a minimum you would need two keystrokes, one for the X coordinate and one for the Y coordinate.

When you aren't entering information that refers to locations, however, the usefulness of the light pen isn't as great. You can still use it to select from a menu of items, but a single keystroke does that easily too. If you need speed and density, voice input offers an interesting alternative.

Studies indicate that the optimum performance comes from combining several input modalities on one system. This makes sense when you think about the way people communicate. You don't just write letters or talk to someone on the telephone when you have something important or complex to communicate. Restricting yourself wouldn't do the subject justice. Besides, each of these requires special skills and suffers from limitations.

When you are really interested in communicating with someone, you sit them down, talk to them, draw graphs and pictures and wave your arms frantically. It seems odd, therefore, to expect to be able to communicate effectively with a machine (that is even a slower learner in some respects than most people) by limiting our inputs to one or two methods, however effective those methods might be. It doesn't make sense. Yet, that is what has been done. Programmers have traditionally been expected to develop at least marginal typing skills. If they didn't, they couldn't program. Simple, right? Simple, and stupid.

The one thing that has done the most to change this attitude is the growth of computers into new applications; applications that require the operator's full attention; applications that require the operator to keep both eyes on some process while inputting data on that process to a computer; applications in which an operator can't be expected to drag a keyboard and display terminal around with him.

In fact, voice input (as well as other input modalities) have expanded the horizons of computer technology. Voice, in particular, suits computers to whole new worlds of service. Verbex Corp. (formerly Dialog Systems Inc.) has identified nine specific areas that the firm feels can benefit almost immediately from voice-input technology:

- ☐ Financial—bill paying by telephone and funds transfer
- ☐ Retail—order entry
- ☐ Transportation—passenger reservations and information
- ☐ Manufacturing—machine control and data entry
- ☐ Insurance—policy information retrieval
- ☐ Education—class scheduling and information retrieval
- ☐ Government—air-traffic control and direct computer access
- ☐ Security—speaker identification
- ☐ Medical—helping the handicapped and information retrieval

And this list doesn't represent all of the possible applications. It merely presents one equipment manufacturer's idea of the marketplace.

The government has shown a significant interest in this technology. On March 5, 1980, Threshold Technology announced that it had been awarded a one-year contract by the Air Force Systems Command, Rome Air Development Center, to pursue software development leading to continuous-speech recognition. Threshold has already installed one voice-input system at the Aerospace Center of the Defense Mapping Agency in St. Louis. The system allows operators to enter data about reference maps into the computer without removing their eyes from the stereoscopic viewers used to view the map. The system is undergoing tests to see how it compares to the keyboard-entry systems used now.

RECOGNITION ISN'T UNDERSTANDING

Although voice-output technology has matured quite nicely in recent years, voice input has much further to go. There has been a great deal of progress in the field, certainly. It's just that voice input offers such tremendous potential that it might be several years before even the research becomes stabilized.

One of the unfortunate aspects of this lack of stabilization lies in the confused terminology used to describe both equipment and technology. This causes many misconceptions to become associated with the claims of various manufacturers. In particular, three terms need careful examination. They are:

- ☐ Voice response
- ☐ Voice entry
- ☐ Voice recognition.

Voice response means the computer responds to your input with a voice of its own. It doesn't indicate that the computer responds *to* your voice at all. As such, the term doesn't really have anything at all to do with voice-input technology. The confusion arises because some voice-recognizer manufacturers advertise that their unit features voice response. The voice-response portion of the unit, however, has little or nothing to do with the recognition circuitry or technology. Voice response, then, identifies a voice-output device, or the presence of voice-output circuitry in a system.

Voice entry identifies the manner by which data enters into the machine. It specifies voice entry as opposed to keyboard entry, punched-card entry or some other means (one of our input modalities). Although this is an honest-to-computer voice-input term, it isn't precise enough. It doesn't tell us enough about the process or what happens to the data once it has entered the computer. A computer system which converts the analog voice signal into a digital form and then stores it in memory qualifies as a voice-entry system. Thus, any computer with a microphone and some analog-to-digital conversion circuitry can qualify as a voice-entry device. There are products advertised under this heading. You have to check carefully to see if the equipment provides any functions beyond this simple voice entry.

Unfortunately, a number of excellent voice recognizers have been hawked as voice entry devices. A number still are, as a matter of fact.

Voice recognition implies that voice inputs can be identified by the computer system. A simple voice recognizer accepts voice and produces an ASCII-character representation of the spoken word to the computer. In a more sophisticated system each word might trigger a predetermined command sequence the same way that special-function keys on a video terminal do. The significant point is that the voice input gets converted to something that the computer can, with little difficulty, use.

The recognition process is illustrated (in a general manner) in Fig. 5-1. This block diagram proves typical of most commercial recognition systems. The speech filters ensure that, as much as possible, only speech sounds reach the rest of the circuits. Unhappily, there is a lot of noise in our everyday environment which occupies the same frequency band as speech. The filters won't eliminate that kind of noise at all. When you hear, your mind can separate speech from noise, up to a point. Some of the computer programs used in speech recognition can do that too.

The digitizer puts the speech signal into a form the computer can handle. Some recognizers have separate digitizers for each of several band-pass filters. These circuits divide up the speech energy into separate frequency ranges. This is called spectrum analysis, or a spectral analysis. Whether the device uses several digitizers or just one, however, the microprocessor still winds up with a digital representation of the speech signal.

DRAWING CRAZY PATTERNS

Each word can be represented as a different digital pattern. The pattern for most words is different enough that the computer can compare the pattern that it gets by digitizing the incoming word to previously digitized words stored in memory. The word in memory that most closely matches the incoming word is said to have been recognized.

Each manufacturer approaches the filtering, digitization and comparison tasks in a different manner, and we will examine some of those strategies when we begin discussing specific equipment. All recognition equipment must perform those jobs, however.

Of the three jobs, the comparison mechanism provides the most variability. This is partly because the microprocessor does the job under software control. There aren't any standard comparison programs. Each application has different requirements. For some jobs, where the vocabulary is quite limited, you might choose to use a simple recognition program that doesn't demand very exacting matches. This would be appropriate in factories where the background noise is quite high and all the operator needs to enter into the system can be expressed in a few words and digits.

Some systems use math-modeling techniques that can easily get out of hand—the researchers keep adding just one more refinement until it takes a mainframe computer to execute the program. This not only makes the total system a bit on the expensive side, but also tends to make the system's response times too slow for many applications. The mainframe is much

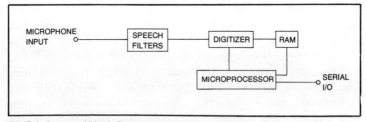

Fig. 5-1. A general block diagram for voice recognition.

faster than smaller computers, to be sure, but the programs tend to be math intensive. Performing a large number of calculations creates bottlenecks in the system.

A term you'll hear associated with recognition equipment is automatic speech recognition (ASR). It isn't clear why the word automatic is included. There isn't much call for manual speech recognition. But it is. The ASR systems fall into three general categories: continuous, segmented and isolated speech recognition.

Isolated-word recognizers are the easiest to define. They recognize individual words (or utterances) separated by short pauses. The pause helps the recognizer find the end of one word and the beginning of the next. The term "word" can be slightly misleading here. For all isolated-word recognizers, the term applies to whatever speech distinctions you've established. A short phrase can be a word in the context. A word comprises whatever fits into the time allotted for a word. This is why most recognizer's data sheets use the term utterance rather than word. So a data sheet that specifies that a unit recignizes 16 utterances is saying that it recognizes 16 different items (digits, words, noises, anything).

The pause that separates utterances varies depending on the recognition system. Usually it will be more than 100 milliseconds to ensure that the system doesn't confuse the pause between words with pauses sometimes occuring within words. A standard value for pauses is 200 milliseconds, or one-fifth of a second.

The utterance itself has limits. If it is less than 200 milliseconds long, the recognizer won't hear it. The maximum length for most units runs about two seconds. Any utterance between 200 milliseconds and two seconds long, therefore, can be used as a word. If you are using phrases, however, you have to be sure they don't contain any pauses longer than 200 milliseconds.

Segmented-speech systems are isolated-word recognizers that don't put any restriction on the pauses. You can group isolated words together; speak them quickly. This means you can speak a string of digits, for example, in rapid succession, without having the recognizer getting jumbled up.

Continuous-speech systems aren't available commercially. In fact, the only systems using continuous recognition are those you'll read about later in this chapter. These recognizers hear as rapidly as you can speak and you make no concessions to the fact that you're talking to a machine instead of a person. Ideally, that is. Practice might be quite different.

Recognizers exhibit two other classifying characteristics. They are either *speaker dependent* or *speaker independent*. Most commercial systems are speaker dependent. This means that if you want to use the system, it must be trained to understand the way you say each word. Most speaker-dependent systems have a switch which allows you to put them into a train mode. The training consists of the machine listening to the way you say each word in the system vocabulary and storing a reference pattern, or template, in memory that is associated with each word. These patterns are the output of the digitizer we talked about earlier. Typically you'll have to repeat each word a few times before the machine can build a pattern that will recognize the word reliably. This is because the recognizers average several patterns to create the reference pattern. This helps iron out some of the variations it will see in the way you say any given word under differing conditions.

As you might guess, because the recognizer simply accepts whatever you say as the reference pattern, you don't *have* to say the word it expects to hear at all. For demonstration purposes, Lloyd Rice, of Computalker Consultants, programs his system to prompt for "hello" and accept "how are you?" Thus, the demonstrator and the machine appear to carry on a dialog. You might find it relaxing to train the recognizer to accept "garbage" when it expects the digit "one." Your imagination is the only limit. The only drawback to such game playing is that the prompts lose their meaning completely. You have to remember what it is you programmed the recognizer to hear. If you forget you'll have to retrain the system. Not a disaster, but inconvenient to say the least.

THE RECOGNIZERS YOU CAN BUY

Figure 5-2 shows one of the first board-level recognizers to come on the market—Interstate Electronics' Voice Recognition Module (VRM). The VRM is designed to let you build voice-input

Fig. 5-2. The Voice Recognition Module (courtesy of Interstate Electronics).

capability, voice recognition technology, right into your own microcomputer-controlled system.

The block diagram shown in Fig. 5-3 illustrates the operation of the VRM. A bank of 16 bandpass filters divide the speech input into 16 discrete channels. Interstate Electronics feels that these channels provide a high degree of recognition accuracy. They selected filter parameters (characteristics) that allow them to get the most information from the speech signal. Studies indicating the frequencies that contained the most spectral information resulted in the choice of frequencies for the filters. After all, if the filter isn't placed within the range of speech energy, it is wasted.

Note the train/recognize switch. This tells you that the VRM is a speaker-dependent device. The size of the reference-pattern RAM space determines the VRM's vocabulary size to a large extent. The vocabulary size and type of interface that comes with the board help establish its model number. A Model 40, for example, provides a 40-word vocabulary and comes with a parallel interface. If you buy from 500 to 999 units, each one will cost $1350.

The Model 102 offers 100 words in its vocabulary. It costs $2255 if you only want one; in quantities from 500 to 999 you'll pay $1845 for each board.

Interstate Electronics' work in voice recognition didn't begin with the VRM. The firm has successfully marketed its Voice Data Entry System (VDES) for some time. The VDES comprises a big brother to the VRM. It can support up to four users, all talking at the same time. Each user gets a vocabulary of 200 to 250 words. If you want to restrict the system to one verbal operator, the vocabulary can contain as many as 900 words.

To help you use the system, Interstate Electronics developed a special operating system, called VOICE (voice-oriented core executive). It is this software that makes the system respond correctly to voice input. You determine what that response is. You can dictate the action you want associated with a specific command and, once that command is recognized, the system will take the appropriate action every time.

One use of the software is to create a form. An operator, such as the one shown in Fig. 5-4, doesn't have the time to spend guessing how to enter inspection data into the computer. Using VOICE intelligently, a system designer can establish a series of prompts, each one leading through a different course of action. If there is nothing wrong with the board that operator is inspecting,

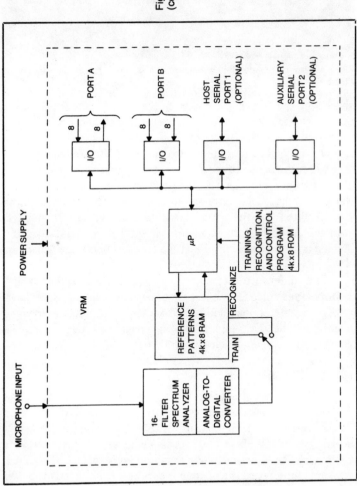

Fig. 5-3. The VRM's block diagram (courtesy of Interstate Electronics).

97

Fig. 5-4. Inspectors enter data without using their hands (courtesy of Interstate Electronics.)

she might say "good." The system then gets ready for the next unit. If the board has a problem, however, the system could prompt by asking, "where is damage: top, edge, bottom?" Thus, the operator is reminded of the vocabulary words (top, edge, bottom) that will make sense to the system at this point in the inspection. This approach also serves to standardize reporting methods. Rather than have an operator mention that the etch of the circuit is slightly lifted "by the corner," she would say, "top; upper left corner." An extremely complex circuit board might even be divided up into quadrants so that the operator could say "quadrant 1,3."

The difference between the board-level VRM and the system-level Voice Data Entry System is one of intent. If you have a large computer installation and want to add intelligent voice input, you'll need a complete system; to build a product that uses voice input you should look at board-level products.

LOW-COST RECOGNITION

Interstate Electronics is not the only firm that's chasing the star of low-cost board-level voice entry. Heuristics Inc. makes a line of products that fall into this category as well. The SpeechLab board recognizes 32 to 250 words—it takes 4K bytes of your computer's RAM for each 32 words in the vocabulary. The block diagram of the board is shown in Fig. 5-5. It is intended for S-100

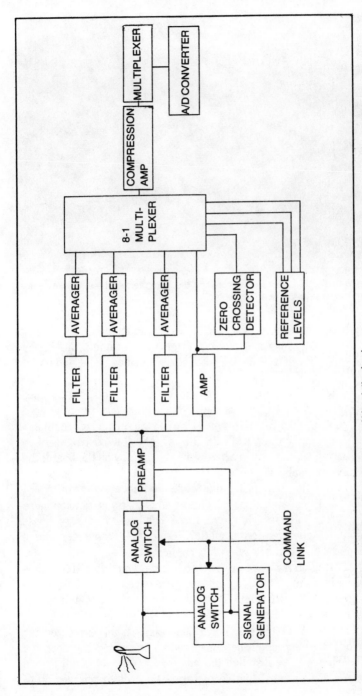

Fig. 5-5. The block diagram of the Speechlab (courtesy of Heuristics Inc.).

99

Fig. 5-6. The Heuristics 5000 converts the dumb terminal into a voice-entry terminal (courtesy of Lear Siegler Inc.).

bus-based computer systems. These microcomputers, usually 8080 or Z80 microcomputers, originally occupied the hobby markets, but have moved into small business and industrial applications.

The recognizer comes in two models: The Model 20-S comes with a ROM-based program for 2-MHz Z80s that provide word recognition. Your BASIC program can call the recognizer routine.

Remember the VRM's 16 filters? The low-cost SpeechLab uses two filters. The more hardware you employ on the board, the more you must be willing to pay.

Heuristics also makes the Model 50 SpeechLab. This board uses functional signal-processing modules that you can configure with your software. It offers three bandpass filters, a linear amplifier, compression amplifier, 6-bit A/D converter and a beeper. This fits the heavier-duty applications.

A step up from the SpeechLab boards, you'll find Heuristic's 500 (Fig. 5-6). This single-board recognizer transforms Lear-Siegler's ADM-3A Dumb Terminal into a voice-actuated video-display terminal. Both Lear Siegler and Heuristics sell the board, which costs $2000 in single-unit quantities. At this price you get the board, a microphone headpiece and a 5-foot connecting cord.

When you've installed the board in a terminal you'll have a voice-entry terminal that recognizes 64 words or phrases up to three seconds long (each). The terminal listens continuously and features an automatic gain control on all audio inputs.

The falling price of voice-recognition equipment is quickly making it possible to buy a "standalone" recognizer at a price that suits the world's largest potential computer marketplace—personal computers. Toward that goal, Scott Instruments has arranged to make it possible to economically put ears on Apple, PET and TRS-80 computers. The firm's VET (voice-entry terminal) series (Fig. 5-7) costs only $895, plugs into a computer's I/O

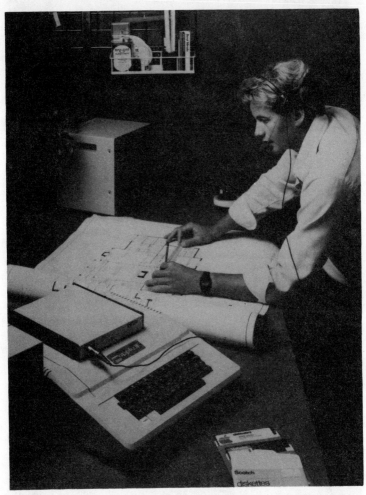

Fig. 5-7. The VET/2 gives personal computers voice-entry capability (courtesy of Scott Instruments).

Fig. 5-8. the Cognivox offers low-cost recognition (courtesy of Voicetek).

port and is immediately ready to begin training to recognize 40 words. By storing word patterns (templates) on a floppy disk, and doing a little creative programming, you can overlay vocabularies. Restricting possible word choices by context allows up to 17 vocabularies to be active for one speaker. That means it will recognize a total of 680 words that you speak. At any one time, however, the system recognizes 40 words.

A demonstration diskette comes with the unit to ensure that you get started correctly. The programs on the diskette help with speaker training and illustrate how to write application programs in BASIC that let you put the recognizer to good use.

Although the VETs require training to recognize the way in which speakers will say each word, Brian Scott, president of the Scott Instruments has developed some strategies that serve to increase recognition speed and accuracy while offsetting the need to train the system separately for every speaker. The firm doesn't claim speaker *independence* for its VETs—simply that it might not be necessary to retrain the system for a new speaker if the new speaker's speech patterns are sufficiently similar to those of the person who trained the unit.

The technique that allows more than one person to use the same set of templates is called variance weighting. It's a software strategy that places the emphasis of the analysis on word parts that don't vary too much from one speaker to another. The system attempts to vocus on what was said rather than the manner in which the word was spoken.

Scott has introduced a second recognition technique that speeds the recognition process. The first thing a VET does when it receives a new word is count the number of syllables in the word. It can then compare this syllable count with similar counts for all the words in its vocabulary. Obviously, if the syllable count is wrong, the words won't match, so the VET eliminates those words from its candidate list before it does any other analysis. Eliminating comparisons means the process goes much faster. Scott estimates the system can typically eliminate from one-third to one-half of its vocabulary for each comparison.

The final decision, the method by which the VET selects the word match, comes from a differencing algorithm. The software looks for features in the input word that differ from those in the reference word being compared at the moment. After comparing each word (the ones that passed the syllable-count test, of course) to the input word, the one with the best match (lowest score) is considered to be the word. There are still a couple of conditions, however. The match gets thrown out unless the differencing score is below 150 points and the word that scored second best is at least 10 points higher. If the word "five" scored 140 points and the word "nine" scored 160 points, for example, then "five" would be a clear choice. If "nine" scored 145, or if "five" scored 150 points, the decision wouldn't be clear enough for the VET to accept.

When too many words don't get accepted, you can display the algorithm's output to see what is going wrong. If you train the recognizer to understand the way you say a given word, yet the scores for that word are borderline, you might need to retrain the system. It might also be that you've just been using the system too long and your voice needs a rest.

Another manufacturer who supplies voice recognition equipment for personal computers is Voicetek. Its Cognivox SR-100 recognizes 32 words and comes with a microphone, a cassette with the necessary software and a user manual for only $119. The unit, shown in Fig. 5-8, works with PET, AIM-65 and Sorcerer computers. TRS-80 version costs $149 and includes a speaker and audio amplifier.

Cognivox uses a nonlinear pattern matching strategy that affords it a high level of recognition accuracy.

Centigram sells its Mike recognition hardware as a standalone unit that acts as an intelligent terminal, complete with recognition electronics, power supply, keyboard and interface. It also sells the bare recognizer board. In either configuration you can order an optional voice-response system that completes the package.

Mike, as a complete system, looks like the diagram in Fig. 5-9. It can learn and recognize 16 isolated words or short connected phrases. An expanded-recognition memory option lets you store 12 sets of 16-word vocabularies.

The voice-response system allows you to prerecord up to eight seconds of messages for controlled playback. You can buy an expanded response memory option that will add additional response.

The single-board version of Mike costs $1750. Voice-response adds another $750. A fully equipped standalone system, with both recognition and response (the Model 4700), costs $3500. And this isn't the end. Now the firm offers recognition boards specifically designed to suit the recognition needs of PDP-11 users and cost only $1000 to $1250. The UniMike (so called because it works over the Unibus) represents Centigram's commitment to filling the recognition requirements of industrial OEMs.

SPECIALIZED SYSTEMS

The voice-recognition equipment you'll see marketed might be quite specialized compared to the systems we've discussed so far. For commercial applications, a number of good reasons exist for cutting down on the flexibility of a system and concentrating on doing a particular job.

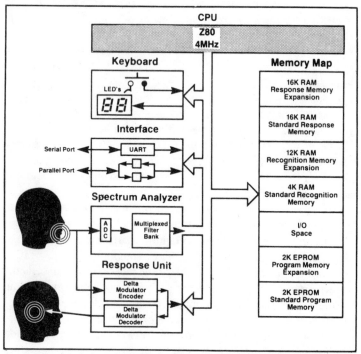

Fig. 5-9. The block diagram for Mike (courtesy of Centigram Corporation).

Consider the recognizers that must be tucked away inside other products, for example. Toshiba America Inc. has a recognizer, called the Acoustic Remote Controlled System (ARCS), that it uses in consumer products. In 1980, at the Consumer Electronics Show, Toshiba introduced a television set and a high-fidelity sound system that both respond to voiced commands.

By employing isolated-word recognition and restricting the vocabulary to the minimum words necessary, Toshiba reduced the task somewhat. Choosing to make the system speaker dependent also relieves some of the burden. The system still represents a remarkable achievement, however. The stereo has 17 commands that you can train it to recognize. These few commands provide control over volume, tone, cassette-tape transport and all other functions. In the television set you need 30 commands to pick a channel, set the volume and tune the set.

Another place that voice equipment has begun turning up is at the banks. These sophisticated systems often use similar restrictions on vocabulary to maintain a high level of recognition accuracy. If the equipment doesn't prove to be error free, the banks and other financial institutions can't afford to use it no matter how efficient it is.

They get the accuracy they need, too. At Chase Manhattan Bank, N.A., for example, a voice system from Interstate Electronics allows operators to enter data directly into a large main-frame computer. During its system-evaluation phase, testers reported only one error in 10,000 transactions.

TAKING WORDS OUT OF ISOLATION

Threshold Technology has spent a great deal of time and energy developing systems that suit practical application in data-entry environments. In one such system, the VNC-200, the firm has established a method of using voice input to enter data from a print or drawing for numerical-control applications. This system lets the operator concentrate on the print and enter the data while reading it.

The Threshold 500 serves as a direct replacement for a keyboard. You can unplug a keyboard from its RS-232C or 20-milliamp current-loop interface and connect the voice unit in. It accepts from 32 to 220 words and phrases and communicates them to a host computer so that the computer can't tell whether they came from a keyboard or voice unit. The operator knows, however.

Not content with the unnatural limitations that isolated word recognition imposes on speech, Threshold's engineers developed Quiktalk. The problem with isolated recognition is twofold. When you are entering a long string of digits, you'll tend to push the words close together, too close for conventional recognizers to identify the pause between them. The second problem is that if you must speak in a halting manner, you're more likely to make a factual mistake. Quiktalk solves the problem by allowing segmented speech. A buffered input accepts individual words at 180 words per minute—a normal speech rate.

Nippon Electric Company Ltd. (NEC) attacked the isolated-speech problem from a slightly different perspective. The firm's DP100 makes the time axis of both the incoming utterance and the reference patterns nonlinear. This warping process eliminates time differences between the two patterns and reduces the task of computing the end of one word and the beginning of another. NEC calls this technique connected-speech recognition. Don't confuse this with continuous-speech recognition, now. We'll discuss that shortly. In the DP100, each word must still be recognized individually. The firm has simply offered another way of separating words. Although you needn't pause between words, the system restricts you to a maximum of five words per sentence, and you must pause for 0.4 to 2.5 seconds between sentences. The unit has two audio-input channels. You can share 120 words worth of storage between the two channels. You can give each channel a 60-word vocabulary, or you could use all 120 words for one channel.

Since we've come so close to it, let's take a look at the problems of continuous-speech recognition. The task proves so complex that IBM has established an entire research group to explore it. At IBM's Thomas J. Watson Research Center (Yorktown Heights, NY) this group, headed by Dr. Fredrick Jelinek, has shown that recognizing speech at normal conversational rates might be possible. The group uses an IBM 370 Model 168 computer to perform the analysis. The speaker must sit in a quiet room. The speech came from a special vocabulary. But the system did recognize continuous speech.

The computer analyzes the speech in several sophisticated ways (Fig. 5-10) all at the same time. It transcribed speech composed of sentences randomly created from a 1000-word vocabulary called the laser patent text. The text was chosen because its words had no special significance to the computer. The

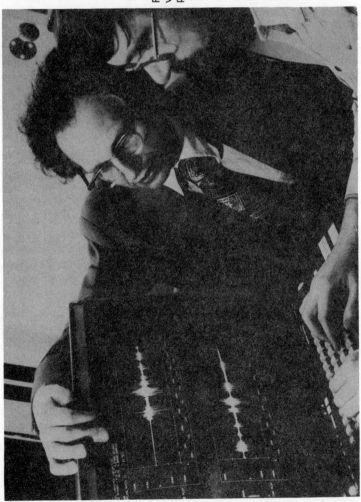

Fig. 5-10. IBM scientists analyze voice patterns (courtesy of IBM Corporation).

speaker read the text at a normal reading pace. The system managed to transcribe the text with a 91 percent accuracy.

In developing the recognition strategies used in this test, Dr. Jelinek's group examined all the speech processes involved—sentence production, pronunciation and signal processing.

IBM's recognition effort is still strictly experimental. Several important obstacles are in the way of making this system a reasonable product the firm can take to market. The obstacles fall into three categories: price, restricted vocabulary and response time.

It would be an understatement to say that IBM's system is expensive. The quiet room alone costs more than even the more expensive isolated- and segmented-word recognizers, never mind having to buy a System 370 computer. The uses that you could put a transcription system to probably don't justify this kind of expense. And then there are the other restrictions.

The vocabulary restrictions don't suit general use. They are, unfortunately, necessary at this point. To make the system truly recognize continuous speech, context and syntax checking had to be eliminated. It has to be possible for the speaker to speak nonsense and be understood. Continuous speech implies that there are no rules. This makes the word-matching job quite complex. So far, the idea of expanding the vocabulary beyond 1000 words doesn't look practical.

Expanding the vocabulary not only complicates the recognition task, it makes it take longer too. It makes sense that it takes longer to compare one thing to a million things than it does to compare it to 1000 things. And even comparing only to 1000 things can take a long time. IBM's recognition system has a 200:1 response time. That means that if the speaker says a 25-word sentence in 30 seconds, he won't be able to see the system print it out for 100 minutes. It could take some time to dictate a letter at that rate, even if the vocabulary was large enough to do the job.

Dr. Jelinek does expect that discoveries will ease the path. He visualizes the ideal recognition system as accepting unrestricted speech from any speaker, providing instantaneous transcriptions and offering an immediate verbal-editing feature for correcting mistakes. Your mistakes, or the recognizer's.

LISTENING TO ANYONE

At Verbex Corporation, researchers determined that restrictions on *what* was said to a computer were less important than the

Fig. 5-11. The Model 1800 voice-entry unit (courtesy of Verbex Corporation).

restrictions on *who* said it. Speaker dependency, to Verbex, was the major obstacle that kept voice input out of the commercial marketplace.

It should be no surprise, therefore, that Verbex's entry to this market comprises a syste.n operating without operator training. The system still uses reference templates, but it uses very special ones. Verbex gathered a cross section of user voices—male and female, northern and southern—that it used to generate a composit reference pattern that doesn't care *how* you say the word, as long as you say a word it knows. The firm occasionally has to fine tune the templates for use in a geographical region, but not often.

Along the route to speaker independence, the firm made a few concessions. The system's vocabulary is quite limited. The Model 1800 (Fig. 5-11) can only store reference patterns for 20 words in 250K bytes of memory. On the other hand, it will handle up to eight users at the same time.

This doesn't seem to be a problem. Verbex's studies show that most voice-input installations don't require even 20 words. One factor that helps the system minimize the recognition vocabulary's restrictions is the richness of the response unit. Verbex manufactures its own voice-response system. Initially the firm used an optical disk to store prerecorded messages. The system sounded uneven. It could take up to 600 milliseconds for the right word to come around on the disk. The unit's choppy speech turned people off.

Now Verbex uses a solid-state response system that provides up to 280 vocal prompts. With the computer so chatty, the system gives the illusion that it recognizes far more words than it actually does.

These systems aren't positioned at the low-cost end of the market. A typical installation, such as the one shown in Fig. 5-12, costs between $60,000 and $130,000. Yet, speaker independence makes computer access available to anyone who has a telephone. Every phone becomes a computer terminal. The block marked "data interface" could be any computer system. But the place you're most likely to see it connected is a pay-by-phone system that allows you to call your bank and have your bills paid for you.

PICKING A RECOGNIZER

As you have seen, there are a multitude of manufacturers, each with a different answer, or set of answers, to the problem of finding the voice recognizer you need. You must decide, eventually, what makes a recognizer the right one for your application.

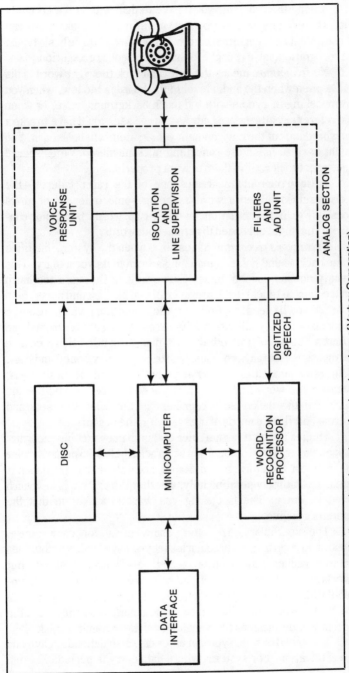

Fig. 5-12. A block diagram for the pay-by-phone type of system (courtesy of Verbex Corporation).

Among the problems you'll have to deal with is the certainty that whatever recognizer you use, it *will* make mistakes. We call these mistakes recognition errors. They come in three basic types: no recognition, false recognition and extraneous recognition.

No recognition means the unit can't pick the right word. This can happen when the audio level to the board is too low, when you are speaking in a room with too much background noise, or when the reference patterns are bad. As you can see, you'll have to take a long hard look at the environment your system will be used in. You might have to use noise-cancelling microphones or other special equipment to get any of them to work properly.

False recognition describes one of the rarer failures—the recognizer identifies a word as being some other word in its vocabulary. If the situation involves two words becoming confused, you might only need to retrain both words.

Extraneous recognition takes place when the system identifies some background noise as matching a word in its vocabulary. This usually doesn't happen unless you've trained the word too much (more than 10 times) in the presence of that background noise.

So you'll need to find out the conditions you'll use the recognizer in, as well as its ability to resist and recover from these failures. Some of the other recognizer considerations involve recognition accuracy, vocabulary size, data-entry speed and cost. You aren't looking for the system that's best in all these areas, because you won't find one. The ideal recognizer will be the one that, like the dedicated recognizers in the television sets and stereos, fulfills the needs of the system at the best price.

Studies indicate certain rules of thumb in evaluating recognizers, however. Word recognition accuracies below 95 percent cause the operator to get frustrated. Rapid, accurate data entry depends on the operator cooperating fully, whether the system is keypunch or voice entry. The last thing you want is a system that the operators dislike.

The vocabulary size offers many areas for compromise. Nested, or overlayed, vocabularies let you have large vocabularies without reducing recognition speed very much, if at all. But overlaying will take its toll in software overhead. Small vocabularies, if they are large enough to do the job, generally provide the best performance. Remember that in many ways the size of the vocabulary determines the complexity of the recognition task.

The speed at which you can enter data also depends heavily on the application. For systems where data entry is periodic, as in a quality control station, there's no real need for extra circuitry to reach beyond the limits of conventional isolated-word systems. For zip code sorting, or other applications where you might reel off strings of digits rapidly, high-speed techniques become vital.

The cost of the system will play an important role if your final product is to be a data terminal or other low-cost item. You can't afford to spend over $2000 for a recognizer for a $4000 terminal.

On the other hand, Verbex's $60,000-and-up price tags aren't out of place for the service they provide for megabuck computer systems. One of Verbex's customers estimates that the voice unit saves his firm as much as $25 million every year. That's not a bad return on the investment.

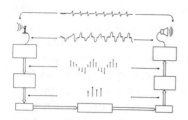

Chapter 6

Second, Adding A Voice
To Your Microcomputer

You should realize by now that voice synthesizers and recognizers come in many forms and sizes. They range from big systems, such as Interstate Electronics Corporation's Voice Data Entry System (Fig. 6-1), which acts as a self-contained intelligent peripheral, to single integrated circuits. Certainly, with this broad range of available devices, there's one just right for your microcomputer system.

The synthesis end of things offers you the most choices, the greatest flexibility. If you can't find a board or box that does exactly what you want—the way you want it done—you can build your own custom synthesizer. It isn't a difficult job. *And you don't even have to buy a voice chip!* There are plenty of other techniques for giving your computer the gift of gab.

FROM TELECOMMUNICATIONS TO YOU

Communicating over long-distance networks such as telephones can cause problems in analog systems. The greater the distance, the higher the noise level. Above a certain level (different in every system) the noise can't be separated from the signal anymore. Unfortunately, the kinds of noise a telephone system generates share many characteristics with speech signals. Low-pass filters can help reduce the amount of high-frequency hissing masking the speech, but they don't do anything at all for noise that falls within the 300-Hz to 3kHz bandwidth of speech.

Digital systems don't have these problems. It's a simple task to separate noise from digital signals. Digital equipment costs less

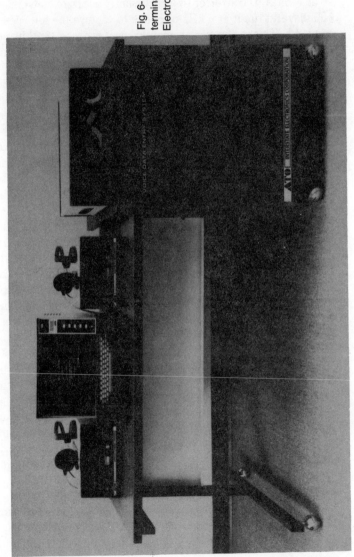

Fig. 6-1. An intelligent voice terminal (courtesy of Interstate Electronics).

to build and maintain than analog systems, too. This has resulted in a lot of research into schemes that convert voices into digital data streams and back again. You can take advantage of this technology to add a voice to your computer.

The most straightforward approach to converting analog to digital is to use an analog-to-digital converter. That seems simple enough until you look at the speech signal a bit more closely. If you use an 8-bit A/D converter to provide fairly accurate conversion, you'll have to run it at 6 kHz or above to capture the full speech bandwidth. This means your computer must process 48K bits per second in order to keep up with the converter. A 48K-byte personal computer system could store eight seconds of speech in its memory—if it had no other programs in memory at the same time. But you can't run the computer without an operating system. And you'll need a program to handle this speech input. It doesn't seem too practical.

The concept is sound, however. In fact, most semiconductor manufacturers serving the telecommunications market offer a device that is little more than this. The circuit is termed a codec (coder-decoder) and it furnishes an analog-to-digital and digital-to-analog converter in the same package.

The codec samples the incoming audio signal at 8 kHz; thus it can pick up smaller variations in the audio signal than our 6 kHz example can—it provides better quality digitization. There's a price, however. The higher sample rate produces more data for any given period of time, and this data must be stored in memory. The 8 kHz encoding scheme uses more memory than the 6 kHz scheme would.

The block diagram shown in Fig. 6-2 illustrates how such a codec-based system would function. If you use Mostek's MK5116 codec, the quality of the digitization is improved even further by the chip's built-in compander (compressor-expander). This circuitry accommodates an input signal with wide fluctuations in amplitude. The range of these fluctutations, called the dynamic range, is made more manageable by compression—the small-amplitude signals are amplified while the large-amplitude signals are held constant. The digital signal is converted back to analog (speech) and the expander reverses the process, restoring the normal amplitude variations back to the signal.

Using the codec to design your speech synthesizer allows you to take advantage of one other part that will simplify your design compared to other approaches. Rather than design and build a low-pass input filter (to keep out unwanted noises), you can use a pulse-code modulation filter, such as the MK5201. This chip is specially designed to provide low-pass filtering for the MK5116 codec.

If you are intending to add a speech synthesizer to your STD-bus computer, the block diagram shown in Fig. 6-3 might suit your purposes well. This circuit uses the codec technology that we discussed to provide an STD-bus system with natural-sounding speech. The circuit's interface lets the synthesizer operate in the interrupt mode.

The MK3881 programmable input/output (P10) chip interfaces the speech circuitry to the computer's bus. One of the PIO's two ports talks to the computer system's serial-to-parallel and parallel-to-serial converters, while the other port interrogates the microphone and option switches. This second port also oversees I/O operations and interfaces with the interrupt logic.

When you want to record utterances for later playback, you put a microphone switch in the ON position. The PIO notices the switch is ON and begins looking for 8-bit parallel data from the serial-to-parallel converter. You speak into the microphone; the analog signal gets filtered by the MK5201 low-pass filter—it furnishes an analog signal the codec can handle; the codec encodes the analog signal as a digital representation and passes it to the serial-to-parallel converter.

When you want the circuit to speak, the appropriate message is routed from its RAM storage area (in the computer's memory) to the parallel-to-serial converter. This data gets decoded by the codec, filtered by the MK5201 and sent to the analog output circuitry.

DELTA MODULATION

You can reduce memory requirements for voice digitization by trying a modulation scheme called delta modulation. Modulating

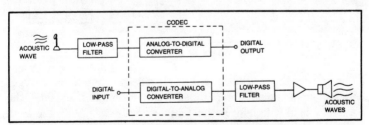

Fig. 6-2. You can use a codec to build voice I/O for your system.

117

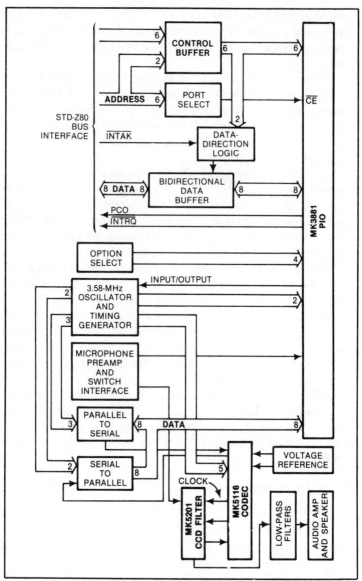

Fig. 6-3. You can use a codec to add speech to an STD-bus system.

the signal means encoding it. The term delta refers to the changes in the input signal's amplitude. Delta modulation encodes the output signal with information that describes changes in the input signal. Thus, you don't need an 8-bit D/A converter. At each sample time, one bit describes the change—up or down. Thus, a 16 kHz sample rate produces 16k bits per second if you use delta modulation, instead of the 128k bits per second that the same rate with a codec would mean.

Figure 6-4 illustrates a simple delta modulator. The comparator detects changes in the input level with respect to the previous input level. The integrator provides the feedback for the comparison. The flip-flop at the comparator's output squares up the pulses and produces a clean digital-data stream. The incoming signal, therefore, starts out like the analog wave shown in Fig. 6-5 (1) and winds up looking like the digital signal (2). Obviously, the faster you run the clock, the smaller the change the system can record. When you can resolve the smallest perceptible changes, you'll have achieved high fidelity. You will also have pushed the clock speed so high that you'll have the same old memory usage problems you had with the codec-based system.

The trick is to find the ideal compromise point. Run the clock fast enough so that the voice sounds intelligible when you play it back through the demodulator shown in Fig. 6-6. Intelligibility is all you are after anyway. For high fidelity you won't want to use a personal computer. You'll be working with at least a 16-bit microcomputer.

Delta modulation does experience a few problems, however. At any reasonable clock rate, its dynamic range has severe

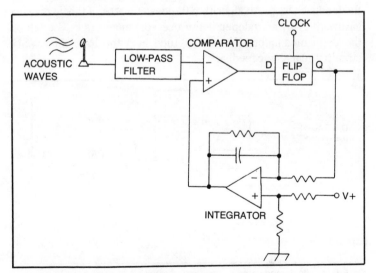

Fig. 6-4. A simple delta modulation input circuit.

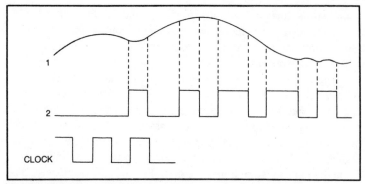

Fig. 6-5. The input signal (1) gets stored as a digital representation (2) of its amplitude changes.

limitations. You can add an external compander, such as one manufactured for recording studios. This will effectively extend the system's dynamic range. But, as long as you build the system from scratch anyway, it's preferable to do things right. Build in the compander function.

When you add a compander to the delta-modulation circuit, its name changes. The circuit is now called a continuously variable slope delta modulator (CVSD). Figure 6-7 illustrates the extra hardware involved in upgrading the previous encoder. The inner delta-modulation loop stays the same. What you will add is the circuitry necessary to adjust the integrator's gain, thus controlling the feedback loop. An algorithm (it doesn't matter if this is done in hardware or by an independent processor) monitors the output of the delta modulator. If the amplitude gets too low, the CVSD circuitry adjusts the feedback.

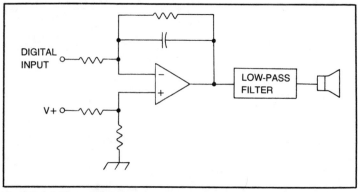

Fig. 6-6. A delta demodulator.

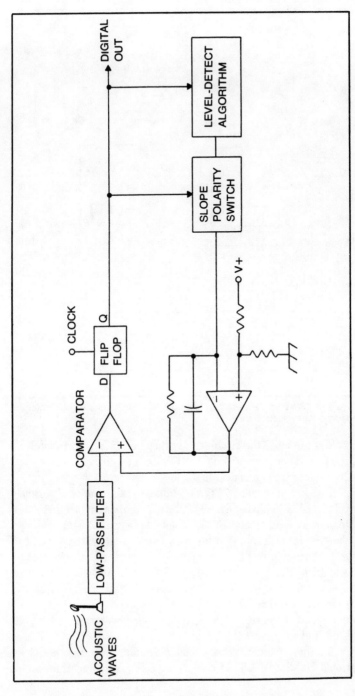

Fig. 6-7. The block diagram of a CVSD encoder.

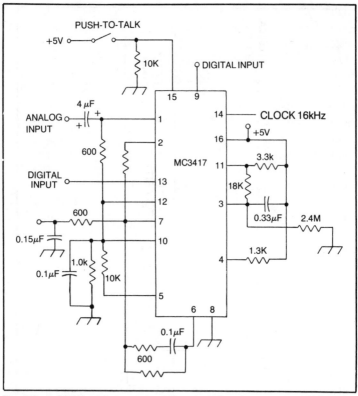

Fig. 6-8. A CVSD system using a Motorola MC 3417 (courtesy of Motorola Semiconductor Products Inc.).

You can build the circuit easier than you think. Fortunately, a number of companies make CVSD integrated circuits, saving you an incredible amount of design work.

The circuit shown in Fig. 6-8 requires only one of Motorola's MC3417 CVSD chips and a few external components to accommodate your system nicely. For high-speed operations Motorola also makes the MC3418, but for memory conserving systems the 3417 works quite nicely. You can operate this circuit at clock rates as low as 9600 Hz. If you set aside a 10k byte memory buffer in your system, you could store over eight seconds of speech in it. Running the circuit at 16 kHz would give you five seconds of speech in the same space. Experiment a bit to see what works best for your system and your ear.

Another vocoder (voice encoder-decoder) uses Harris Corporation's HC-55516 CVSD chip (Fig. 6-9). Although this circuit might look somewhat more complex than the last one and might prove a little harder to build, its speech quality should also be a bit better. Most of the extra circuitry is involved in the output filter. This filter helps to smooth out the speech signal. Thus, you might even be able to run the circuit at a lower clock rate than you could without the filter. The extra circuit-building effort could save system memory. At the very least, it will add to the system's intelligibility. The operational amplifiers scattered throughout the design are specified as Harris 4741s, but you can use any equivalent part.

If you like the idea of delta modulation and its variations, but don't want to get involved in building the whole thing from the ground up, Mimic Electronics can help. Their Mimic Speech Processor (Fig. 6-10) uses a technique the firm's James Anderson feels is "not a CVSD system, and has a number of advantages over CVSD." The system operates at 9600 Hz clock rates. The modulation technique is proprietary, but if you aren't building that portion of the circuit, you won't really care.

You gain one benefit from using the Speech Processor rather than building a CVSD system, besides the fact that you can buy the Speech Processor already built. You can use high-speed mathematical algorithms to perform recognition on the speech input. Anderson has already published papers in *Byte* magazine exploring this application. Other articles will follow. There's no established software for this task yet, but the possibilities are endless. You might write your own.

To use a speech processor, of course, you'll have to connect it to your computer system. The Mimic system connects to many computer systems through a parallel I/O port. If you have a TRS-80, you'll have to buy a special version of the speech processor.

The basic Speech Processor board measures 3 × 5 inches and costs $79. The complete TRS-80 package, including microphone, a speaker with volume control, a +15V power supply and a cable assembly, costs $169.

If you have an S-100 system, you can either buy an S-100 interface for $59 or build it yourself. Mimic Electronics supplies the complete schematic, shown in Fig. 6-11. This gives you an idea of the interface task.

Mimic Electronics also suggests an additional circuit useful for any CVSD or delta-modulation system as well as the Speech Processor. This is the Data Dumper, shown in Fig. 6-12. The Data

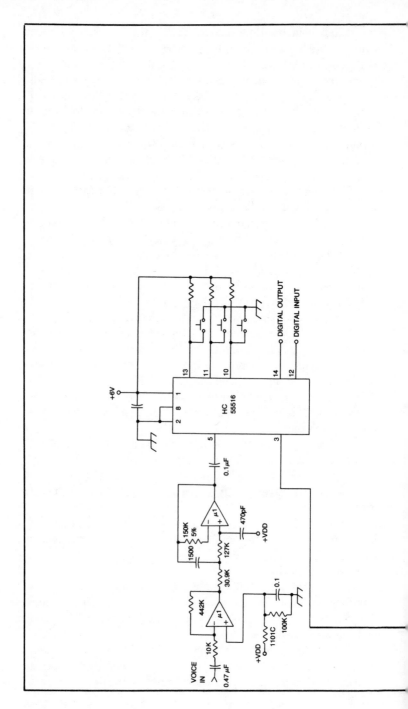

124

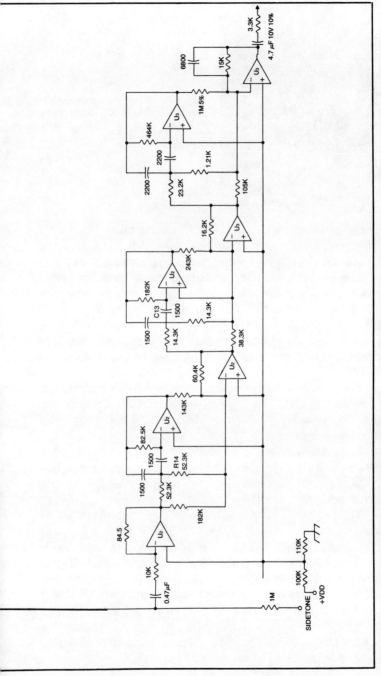

Fig. 6-9. A CVSD system using a Harris HC 55516 CVSD chip (courtesy of Harris Semiconductor).

125

Fig. 6-10. A complete Speech Processor (courtesy of Mimic Electronics).

Dumper reduces the amount of CPU time it takes to output a spoken message. The circuit takes care of the data serialization and timing so the computer can spend that time performing other tasks.

The 4K-byte RAM in the Data Dumper holds up to two seconds of speech with a 16K sample rate. It acts as temporary storage for a message that the hardware has retrieved from ROM or disk storage. The hardware interrupts the computer whenever its RAM is empty and the computer refills it. Thus, the Data Dumper can output phrases longer than two seconds without any difficulty.

The circuit shown was designed for use with the S-100 bus. It depends on the Z80 block-move instruction (OTIR) to transfer the speech data quickly. A single IM 5623 PROM and a few gates decode the output ports.

Block data transfers to Output Port #1 put packed speech data bytes in the RAM. During each output, the data byte is written into the memory location addressed by counter #1. The counter increments after each data-byte output.

The hardware features a replay feature that allows you to output the same message repeatedly. This proves especially handy in the case of beeps. You save the time it takes to continuously reload the RAM with the pattern that will output a beep. This is accomplished when the computer receives a DONE interrupt. If the computer knows the same output should be repeated, it simply activates Output Port #2 to repeat the output process rather than loading new speech data. If the replay isn't wanted, the computer activates Output Port #3 which resets the system. It then loads the new speech data through Output Port #1.

Mimic doesn't make the only speech processor, either. Mountain Hardware offers the Supertalker SD200 (Fig. 6-13) along with data-compression software. This software increases the density at which you store the speech. You can put 100 percent more speech information on a diskette when you use the program than when you work without it. The SD200 digitizes your voice for replay at your choice of 500 bytes per second, 1K byte per second, 2K bytes per second or 4K bytes per second. At the 2K-byte rate you can store about 120 seconds of speech on one 5¼-inch floppy diskette.

In addition to the data-compression software, Mountain Hardware has developed some application programs to help you begin using the unit right away. These application programs might prove to be a large area of competition in the near future. As hardware prices fall and interfaces become standardized, it will be interesting to see the nature of the application programs that come out. To date, most are either simple games or data entry programs.

Voicetek has introduced its Cognivox to provide low-cost voice for a variety of computers. The unit provides digitized storage of up to 52 words in 16K of RAM. The software support includes driver programs (the software that lets the computer run the device) plus two application-program packs, providing eight programs. The programs include VOICETRAP (a voice-operated video game) and VOTHELLO (a voice-input version of OTHELLO).

Optional speech-recognition software takes up 2.5K bytes of RAM and allows you to train the unit to recognize isolated words lasting from 150 millisconds to three seconds.

THE SIMPLE APPROACH

The simplest way to give your computer the voice quality of a Speak & Spell is to buy a Speak & Spell. When you take away the toy's keyboard and case, you can see that it has everything you need in a synthesizer except an interface (Fig. 6-14). Percom Data Company will sell you the interface that plugs the miniature voice into a TRS-80 for about $70; East Coast Micro Products sells a similar interface for 6502-based systems for about $60.

If you aren't content with the Speak & Spell's vocabulary, but like the way it talks (not to mention its $70 price tag), there's a cure for that too. Speek Up Software offers a program that takes up 2k of your computer's memory and lets you type in ASCII characters that represent phonemes—and the computer says them. The software works with the Speak & Spell and either interface, and costs

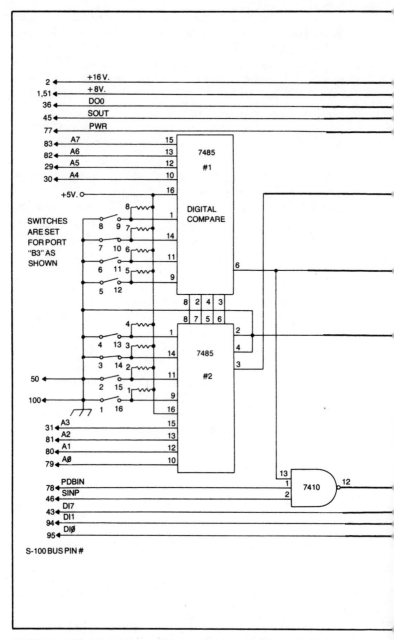

Fig. 6-11. An S-100 interface for the speech processor (Copyright 1979 by Mimic Electronics Company, P.O. Box 921, Acton, MA, all rights reserved. Used by permission.).

128

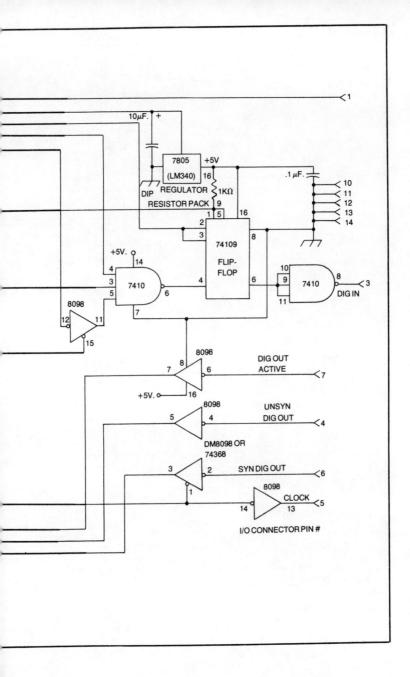

129

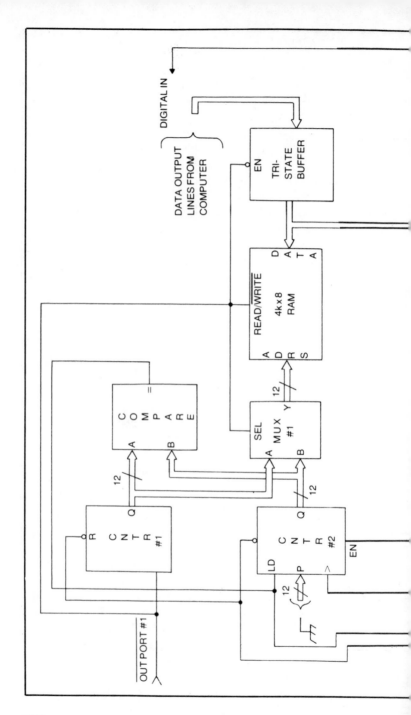

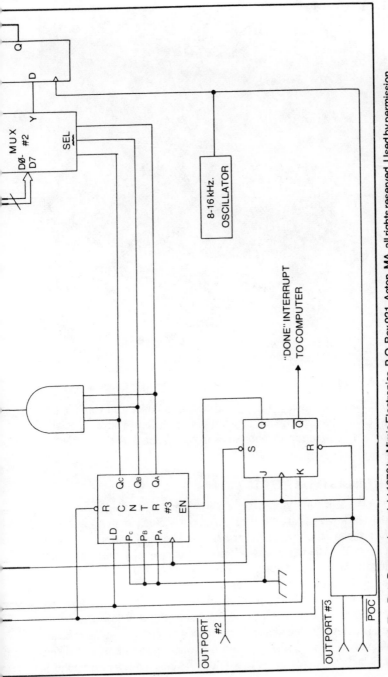

Fig. 6-12. The Data Dumper (copyright 1979 by Mimic Electronics, P.O. Box 921, Acton, MA, all rights reserved. Used by permission.

131

Fig. 6-13. The Supertalker SD200 (courtesy of Mountain Hardware Inc.).

$14.95. If you insist on seeing the source code, you can get the experimenter package for an additional $24.95. If you want to see how the code produces phonemes from the Speak & Spell, it's the only way to go.

PUTTING A SYNTHESIZER TO WORK

Most of the synthesizer boards you'll see advertised claim they work with a particular microcomputer, such as an Apple. This often means the manufacturer has provided an interface that will connect it to that computer. It doesn't necessarily mean you just plug the board in and start using it. In most cases, at the very least you must write some software.

If you buy a board-level synthesizer, you'll usually have to build, if not design, the interface yourself. But this doesn't have to be a problem. In one sense, being forced to do it yourself can be an advantage. The hardware and software that the synthesizer manufacturer would provide wouldn't be tailored for your application. It would, of necessity, be general purpose. A little something for everyone. You'd wind up having to customize the hardware and software anyway; and, if the interface were proprietary, possibly doing it without good documentation. Sometimes schematics of boards you've purchased can be devilishly hard to get ahold of.

Let's take a look at one designer's application and how he incorporated a voice board into it. Gary Gonnella uses amateur radios a lot. Enough to justify getting together with some friends and building a repeater up on one of Southern California's mountains. The repeater serves two purposes. It allows its users to talk long distances with short-range radios and gives each user access to a number of radios from his one mobile unit.

A push-button telephone pad controls the operation of the radios at the repeater site. What was needed was a voice-response system that would inform the operator what the operating parameters were, such as the output frequency.

With so many radios to keep track of, an intelligent control was essential. The microprocessor system running the radios could be upgraded to furnish voice response—at least that was the intention.

The voice system had to always respond, over the radio, to the controlling radio. Additionally, Mr. Gonnella wanted the controller to be able to direct voice output to any of the radios. The overall block diagram is shown in Fig. 6-15.

As you can see, the main purpose in this application was the same as in some commercial order-entry systems—to allow an

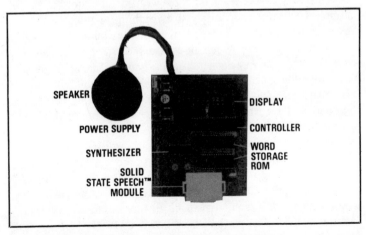

Fig. 6-14. Speak & Spell (courtesy of Texas Instruments Inc.).

operator to control the microcomputer without being near a terminal. Combining tone inputs with voice response, each mobile radio became a computer terminal with limited programming capability.

The controller board was selected before the idea of adding voice response came up. The Z80 evaluation board from SD Systems fortunately provided more than enough computational power for the controller job, even after adding the voice-response tasks.

Telesensory System's Mini Speech Synthesis boards fit the bill for the voice exactly. Each module provides the minimum components necessary to output speech. You select a pre-encoded vocabulary when you pick the module model. The S2A, for example, furnishes a 24-word vocabulary that describes calculator functions. The S2D provides the same words, but in German. You can also speak calculator in Arabic (S2E) and French (S2F). A 64-word ASCII vocabulary describes the ASCII character set, including non-printing keystrokes, such as "upper case" and "control." For the radio application, Model S2B comes with the 64-word standard vocabulary shown in Table 6-1.

All words are spoken in a clear, intelligible voice the manufacturer describes as a male but which sounds more like a Cylon warrior! In the radio application, this was a definite plus. There's less chance of mixing up the voice response system with comments from other operators using the system if the machine sounds like a machine.

The speech modules don't come with an interface. You do get an application note that tells you everything you could possibly care to know about the board, however. This information, and a 20-pin edge connector which gives access to the board's innards, make designing an interface a dream. Figure 6-16 shows the way Mr. Gonnella connected the S2B to his evaluation board/ controller. The Z80 PIO (programmable input/output) resides on the controller board. The rest of the components you'll have to come up with.

This application only requires one of the PIO's two parallel ports. Lines 0 through 5 of port A address the word to be spoken; line A6 strobes the start bit to get the board talking; line A7 provides an input to the controller so it will know when the board is talking and when it isn't. And that's all there is to the hardware. Make sure the buffer on the BUSY line is CMOS—the line won't drive TTL.

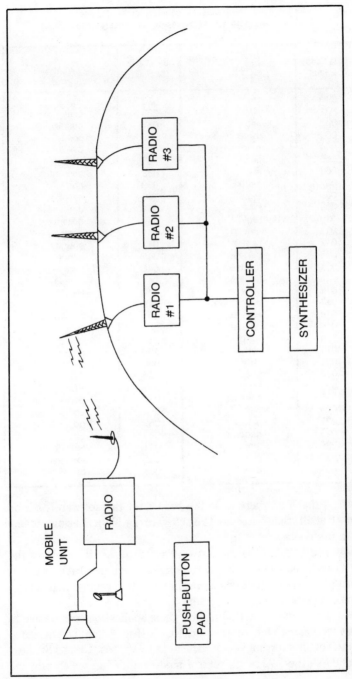

Fig. 6-15. A block diagram of a radio network with its own voice.

135

Table 6-1. The Standard Vocabulary for the Mini Speech Modules Provides 64 Words (courtesy of Telesensory Systems, Inc.).

Data Code (Decimal)	Word	Data Code (Decimal)	Word
000	zero	032	times
001	one	033	over
002	two	034	equals
003	three	035	point
004	four	036	overflow
005	five	037	clear
006	six	038	percent
007	seven	039	and
008	eight	040	seconds
009	nine	041	degrees
010	ten	042	dollars
011	eleven	043	cents
012	twelve	044	pounds
013	thirteen	045	ounces
014	fourteen	046	total
015	fifteen	047	please
016	sixteen	048	feet
017	seventeen	049	meters
018	eighteen	050	centimeters
019	nineteen	051	volts
020	twenty	052	ohms
021	thirty	053	amps
022	forty	054	hertz
023	fifty	055	DC
024	sixty	056	AC
025	seventy	057	down
026	eighty	058	up
027	ninety	059	go
028	hundred	060	stop
029	thousand	061	tone (low)
030	plus	062	tone (high)
031	minus	063	oh

If that's all there is to the hardware, the software can't be much at all, right? Wrong. The software is what makes everything run so smoothly.

The software performs two discrete tasks: it programs the PIO and then handles the voice board through that PIO. The first module would be part of a larger initialization routine that sets up the entire microcomputer system.

To program the PIO for the voice application, you'll have to pay attention to the interface schematic (Fig. 6-16). The first step is to set an interrupt vector. The next two bytes (CF and 80, hex) establish the PIO in its control mode and define which bits will serve as inputs and which will serve as outputs. The 80 (hex) sets bits A0 through A6 as outputs and A7 as an input. The next code line selects the interrupt mode. A B7 (hex) in this case enables the interrupts; a HIGH state will interrupt. The next byte, a 7F, provides the interrupt mask. It masks, or covers over, all but the

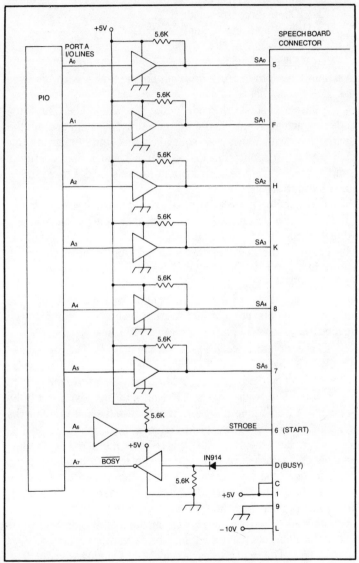

Fig. 6-16. An interface for the speech module, using a P10.

bits that should be monitored. You don't want to waste time looking at lines that won't furnish legal interrupts and you don't want to accidentally trigger an interrupt. The 7F causes the PIO to monitor only bit seven—the only input.

So the initialization routine comprises only five code lines:

☐ Select the interrupt vector (this depends on your system)
☐ PIO into its control mode (CF)
☐ Define input and output lines (80)
☐ Set interrupt mode (B7)
☐ Mask off unimportant bits (7F).

You'll only have to execute this routine one time—each time you use the system, that is.

Figure 6-17 shows the code for the handler module. This is the code that actually controls the synthesizer. You could operate the synthesizer with much less code than this, but remember this comes from an application that does much more than operate a simple voice-response unit. Some of this code takes other functions into account.

The handler uses a data structure, termed a talk buffer (TLKBFR), to accumulate the words that need to be spoken. Actual words aren't stored here, however. What is stored in the talk buffer is the code for the selected word. These codes are shown in Table 6-1. Each entry in the buffer (or table) comprises two bytes. The first byte is the word's code. The second byte tells another routine to which radio (audio channel) to route the response. For a single-channel system, you could eliminate the second byte, thus doubling the effective buffer space.

Three pointers keep track of the buffer. The mnemonic TLKBFR is the address of the start of the buffer space. The buffer takes up the next 256 bytes of RAM. It will, therefore, store up to 128 words. The pointer BYTPTR points to the next word to be spoken; BYTCNT points to the current end of the buffer—it marks the spot behind (following) the last table entry.

When the computer enters this routine, it first performs a few housekeeping tasks. It turns off the interrupts and saves the contents of all the registers. This way, when you return from the voice routine, program execution picks up right where it left off. Otherwise, every time the system interrupted a function to make the board talk, it wouldn't be able to finish what it was doing.

After doing its housekeeping, the processor resets counter/timer CTC1. This acts as the speech circuit's timing element. The address of the talk buffer is then put into the H and L registers and the address of the byte to be spoken gets stuffed into the accumulator. A little manipulation compares the BYTPTR to the BYTCTR. If they are the same, after all, it means the buffer's contents have already been completely spoken. You don't want the board to repeat itself for no good reason. It could be very confusing.

If the buffer's pointer and counter *are* at different locations, indicating the buffer contains some unspoken words, it prepares to speak them. The section called VOICE2 will set up the speech.

VOICE2 first sets the TLKBSY flag. The next six lines of code (6120 through 6160) move the BYTPTR two bytes further through the buffer. Each entry comprises two bytes, so the pointer now points to the code for the word to be spoken next (the next time through this loop, that is, not this time). The next instruction adds the byte pointer to the starting address of the buffer. This puts the address of the word to be spoken now in the H and L registers. That word then gets put into the accumulator.

Every word in the vocabulary of the synthesizer has a code between 00 and 40 (hex). The vocabulary doesn't provide a pause. This system uses a 40 to indicate a pause. Values greater than 40 indicate tones. The tones don't come from the synthesizer, however. The code in lines 6270 through 6510 provides the tones and pauses, using a counter/timer circuit that comes on the Z80 evaluation board.

If the value stored in the accumulator was less than 40, it meant that some word needed to be spoken. The code called VOICE3 handles that. The word's code outputs from the accumulator on PIO lines A0 through A5. The program performs this instruction three times. The first and third times, the strobe is masked off. The second time the code goes out, the strobe (line A6) is on. This ensures that the address lines (A0 through A6) have valid data at the time the synthesizer sees a start strobe.

The speech board's controller takes over at this point, and the board begins talking. The computer's program now jumps to master reset, where the registers are restored to the values they had before we saved them. The interrupts get turned back on (re-enabled) here too. When the speech board finishes speaking the word we gave it, its busy line will generate another interrupt and the entire procedure begins again.

If the Z80 instruction mnemonics don't make it clear to you exactly what's going on, take a look at the flowchart shown in Fig. 6-18. You should be able to write your own program for any computer from this flowchart. The hardware shown will suit any computer that has one port of a PIO available.

```
05830 ;    ******************************
05840 ;
05850 ;  THIS IS THE VOICE HANDLER
05860 ;  AN   H IN THE TABLE IS FOR A SPACE
05870 ;  THE FIRST BYTE IS THE WORD THE SECOND
05880 ;  BYTE IS WHERE THE WORD GOES
05890 ;
05900 ;    ******************************
05910 ;
05920 PINT3    DI                          ; INT'S OFF
05930          EX      AF, AF'
05940          EXX
05950 VOICE1   LD      A, 03H              ; TO RST CTC
05960          OUT     (CTC1), A
05970          LD      HL, TLKBFR          ; START OF TALK BUFFER
05980          LD      A, (BYTPTR)         ; GET PRESENT BYTE CNT
05990
06000          LD      B, A
06010          LD      A, (BYTCNT)         ; GET TOTAL COUNT
06020          CP      B                   ; ARE WE DONE
06030          JR      NZ, VOICE2          ; GET NEXT WORD
06040          LD      A, 00
06050          LD      (BYTCNT), A         ; CLEAR COUNT
06060          LD      (BYTPTR), A
06070          LD      (TALKON), A         ; CLEAR TALK FLAG
06080          LD      (TLKBSY), A         ; CLEAR THE BUSY
06090          JR      VOIEND
06100 VOICE2   LD      A, (TLKBSY)         ; VOICE BUSY
06105          OR      01H
06110          LD      (TLKBSY), A         ; SET FLAG
06120          LD      A, B                ; PUT COUNT IN A
06130          LD      C, A
06140          LD      B, 00
06150          INC     A
06160          INC     A
06170          LD      (BYTPTR), A         ; SAVE NEW VALUE
06180          ADD     HL, BC              ; ADD OFFSET
06190          LD      A, (HL)             ; GET WORD
06200          CP      40H                 ; IS IT FOR SPACE?
06210          LD      B, A
06220          INC     HL
06230          LD      A, (HL)
06240          LD      (TALKON), A
06250          LD      A, B
06260          JR      C, VOICE3           ; ITS NOT?
06270          RRA
06280          RRA
06290          RRA
06300          AND     1CH
06310          LD      B, A                ; SAVE IT IN B
06320          BIT     3, B
06330          JR      Z, BEEP01           ; NOT SET?
06340          SET     2, A
06350          RES     3, A
06360 BEEP01   BIT     2, B
06370          JR      Z, BEEP02
06380          SET     3, A
06390 BEEP02   LD      (TLKDLY), A         ; SAVE IT
06400          DEC     HL
06410          LD      A, (HL)
06420          AND     1FH                 ; MASK UPPER BITS
06430          CP      0
06440          JR      Z, VOIEND
06450          LD      C, A
06460          LD      A, 47H              ; SET UP CTC1
06470          OUT     (CTC1), A
06480          LD      A, C
06490          ADD     A, 3
06500          OUT     (CTC1), A
06510          JR      VOIEND
```

Fig. 6-17. The code for the voice handler.

140

```
06520 VOICE3   AND   3FH           ;MASK OFF STROBE
06530          OUT   (TALK),A
06540          OR    40H           ; ADD THE STROBE
06550          OUT   (TALK),A
06560          AND   3FH           ;STROBE OFF
06570          OUT   (TALK),A
06580 VOIEND   JR    MSTRTN


05770 ;
05780 MSTRTN   EX    AF,AF'        ;MASTER RETURN FROM INT.
05790          EXX
05800          EI
05810          RETI                ; RETURN
05820 ;
```

Fig. 6-17. The code for the voice handler (continued from page 140).

The only additional hardware you'll have to build is the output circuitry. In this application, output amplifiers and filters weren't needed, because the radios provided those features. To use the circuit for operation with a speaker, however, you've got to do a bit more work. Figure 6-19 shows a filter and amplifier circuit that will actually improve the synthesizer's voice quality. The filtering circuitry smooths out some of the transitions (steps) created when you convert a digital signal into an analog signal.

Now you have added a complete synthesizer to your computer system. The same basic approach would work with Telesensory's new Series III modules as well. In fact, the major difference between the Series 2 units and the new Series III boards is that the new ones do more of the work for you. For $395, you get all the functions of the Series 2 units *plus* an on-board (adjustable) amplifier and a standard vocabulary of 119 words. You get a larger vocabulary and can build your system with even fewer parts.

Other firms offer boards that prove easy to use and cost effective, too. Votrax's SPEECH PAC (phoneme access controller) lets you use a simple interface, such as the one we built for the Series 2 board, to try your hand at concatenating phonemes. The board costs $275 and uses the firm's own SC-01 speech chip. You can use SPEECH PAC in two operating modes: prestored words, stored in EPROM can be addressed and called up; you can have direct access to the phoneme-synthesis capabilities of the speech chip.

The block diagram shown in Fig. 6-20 shows the board's prestored word operation mode. You can store up to 255 words in a single 2716 EPROM. A 2532 EPROM holds up to 511 words. Each word furnishes up to eight phonemes. You can, however, combine

141

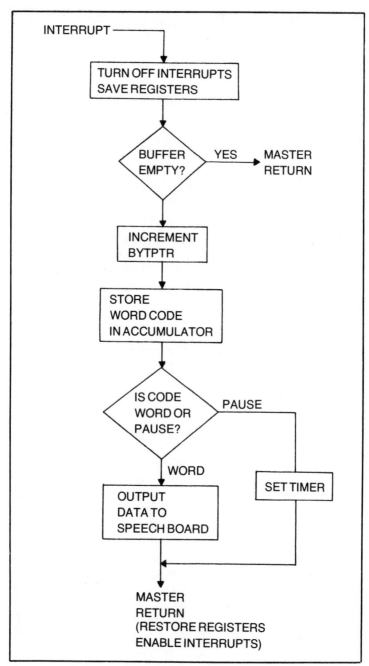

Fig. 6-18. The flowchart for the complete software.

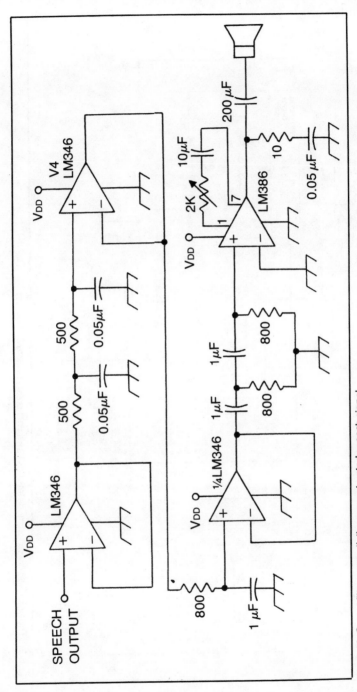

Fig. 6-19. Output filters smooth the reconstructed speech signal.

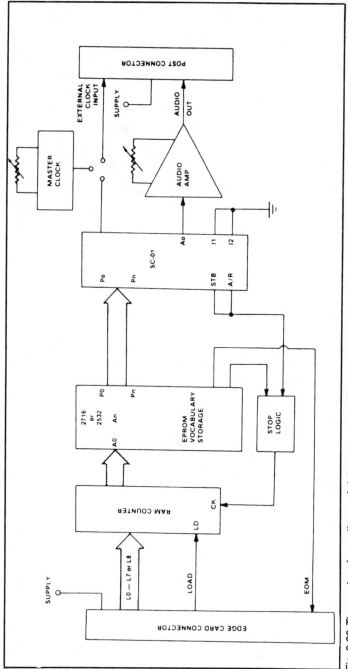

Fig. 6-20. The prestored operation mode lets you use a vocabulary of up to 255 words.

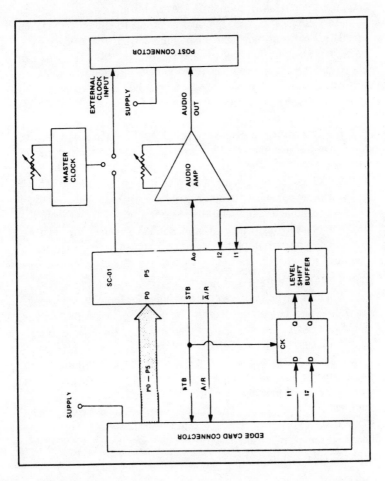

Fig. 6-21. The phoneme-synthesis mode allows constructing any word from phonemes.

word locations to output a single word. Figure 6-21 shows the phoneme-synthesis mode. In either or both operating modes (you can mix modes easily) the board suits a variety of voice-output needs. You can experiment with totally unrestricted speech.

Yet another manufacturer, General Instrument Corporation, has introduced a board that gives you immediate access to its SP-0256 speech chip. The 16K ROM of the chip stores all data and instructions needed to produce 256 discrete sound utterances.

Matsushita has announced marketing plans for a board for its MN1261 voice chip. This board comes without an amplifier, but offers an on-board interface for MN1562 4-bit microcomputer. You might save building any interconnecting hardware at all if you want to use the firm's micro as your computer. For use with another computer, you'll (as a minimum) have to build an adapter.

As you can see, you have many options to choose from; thus you'll have to determine from the beginning what you need from the voice synthesizer. The vocabulary you'll need, the price you can afford and the amount of electronics you wish to add will all play a role. Regardless of the specific choice, however, to make the synthesizer work properly with your computer system you'll have to produce some software.

If Telesensory Systems had provided the software to go with the Series 2 board, they couldn't have foreseen the requirements of the radio system. The code wouldn't fit in with the rest of the system design. In most cases, the voice-response system will have a low priority compared to other system functions. Thus, not only do most manufacturers leave the code writing to you, this is the best and most logical way for things to be. You can ensure you are getting the most out of the system when you write the code yourself. The goal is a complete system.

OTHER CHATTY CHIPS

You still haven't seen the end of ideas for building synthesizers into your computer system, either. Some of the newer signal-processing chips can provide quite interesting voice output.

Consider, for example, Intel's 2920 signal-processor chip. The chip comprises a one-chip audio-bandwidth digital signal processor. It can simulate digital-filter networks to provide a number of signal-processing functions, such as nonlinear transformations. If you remember that formant synthesis isn't really much more than a series of filters excited by a noise source, whose characteristics are varied over time, you'll see where the 2920 fits in as a speech synthesizer.

The filters the chip configures act in much the same manner as the human vocal tract. You must, however, add two important ingredients—a buzz generator, to simulate the vocal chords' vibrations, and a random-noise generator to produce the high-frequency sounds of air turbulence as vocal tract passages are manipulated.

Figure 6-22 shows you how simple a "standalone" synthesizer peripheral can be when you design it around a signal-processor chip. The computer tells the controller which words it wants said; the controller looks in a table, stored in ROM, to see how those words are formed. Each word is broken up into phoneme (basic sound) sequences. The table entries provide the appropriate 2920 instructions to output the desired phonemes at the desired pitch, and for the length of time needed.

Concatenating the phonemes together (stringing them one after the other) causes the speech to be produced in the same way you produce it when you talk. An output filter smooths the analog output from the 2920 to make it sound natural. This is needed anytime you produce audio from digitally stored signals and works exactly like the output filters used in the CVSD and codec systems.

The interesting difference between codec or delta-modulation systems and one formed with the 2920 is that you needn't prerecord the utterances you want said, You will build them completely from digital computer instructions. This is both the advantage and problem to using this approach. It is an advantage because you have an unlimited vocabulary available to you once you have built an adequate lookup table. It's a problem because you have to become familiar enough with the instruction of the 2920 set

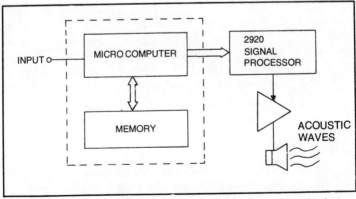

Fig. 6-22. You can use a signal-processor chip for LPC or formant synthesis.

that you can build the speech-data table without having to go through countless trial and error iterations. Once you understand which combinations of instructions produce each phoneme, you must figure out how to dynamically change the pitch and duration of those phonemes without altering the phoneme itself.

This task complete, your software troubles are far from over. To use the peripheral to its maximum, you'll need to write a text-to-speech conversion program. This will let you enter ASCII text and hear it spoken. The flowchart shown in Fig. 6-23 illustrates the operation of the complete software package you'll need.

Intel has just made the design task a bit easier, however. The firm now markets a system-design kit, the SDK-2920 (Fig. 6-24), that includes not only the 2920 chip, but a complete MCS-85 microcomputer system as well. The kit will work like a minidevelopment system by itself, or you can connect it to Intel's Intellec development system to speed up the design cycle. The Intellec provides power for the kit, mass storage, a printer and other peripherals, and access to high-level language tools.

On the board you'll get a keyboard, display, breadboarding area, 2912 PCM line filters, RS232 input/output ports and all the components you need. The complete kit, including assembly manuals and design guides, costs $950. The price does make it a more expensive way to go than the voice boards we talked about previously, but it isn't really intended as just a voice-output board.

If you opt to use the 2920 for your voice experiments, the SDK-2920 provides a great starting platform. Intel offers some additional assistance, too—this time for free. Two application notes provide a great deal of technical details on using the chip for speech applications. To understand the software needed to make the chip really perform, ask for AR-128, "Software Makes a Big Talker Out of the 2920 Microcomputer." For more general information on applying the 2920, request "A General Purpose Formant Speech Synthesizer Using the Intel 2920 Signal Processor." Combining the information on applying the 2920 chip to speech applications with the SDK-2920 kit will give you a fairly comprehensive speech lab.

BEING DISCRETE

Of course, you don't have to use any particular board or even any special *large-scale integration circuit* (LSI) to add speech to a computer. You can build a synthesizer from individual components,

148

using nothing any more complex than a *single-chip operational amplifier* (op amp). For the diehard experimenter, nothing will do but to build from scratch.

And, if you're going to throw away the contemporary chip designs, why not give the synthesis process a fresh approach too? Why emulate a chip with discrete components? What's the gain?

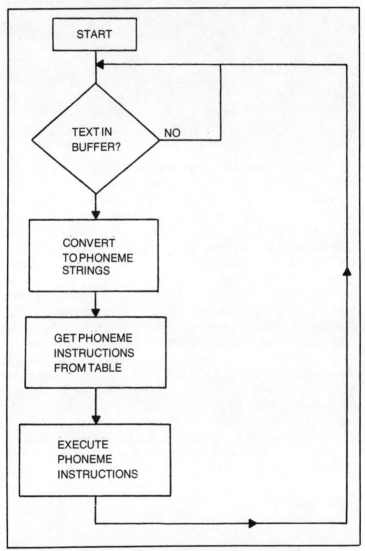

Fig. 6-23. Converting English text into speech is a software task.

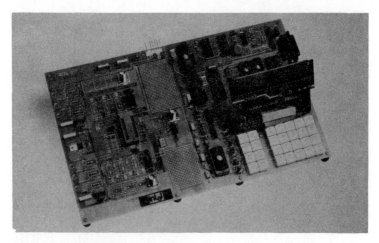

Fig. 6-24. The SKD-2920 board from Intel gives you powerful signal-processing capability on a single board.

You could, for example, take a step back in time and look at the pre-electronic synthesizers. Remember the mechanical Voders we talked about in Chapter 3? One of the major difficulties with such a contraption is its complex operation. But today you don't have to depend on the crude pulleys and levers that frustrated these machine's designers. You might, by applying servo technology borrowed from robotics, develop a unit that would operate reasonably well—and under computer control!

But perhaps mechanics isn't your long suit. There still must be ways to model the human vocal tract that haven't been tried. The problem with experts can sometimes be that they know *too* much. Approach the task with a firm knowledge of your own strengths. If you can't solder, don't spend your life trying to cluge together a microcomputer from scratch. It isn't worth it—certainly not when you can buy them so cheaply. If you are a whiz at throwing hardware together, however, there are some tremendous advantages to building specialized equipment. For one thing, you know what to expect from it. The point is that just because there are a number of products available today, it doesn't necessarily follow that all, or any, of the products use the best (or most efficient) technology.

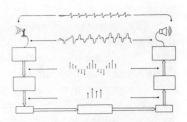

Chapter 7
Some Systems Ahead Of Their Time

Voice technology might sound exciting today—and indeed it is—but the products you've already heard about just scratch the surface. You haven't even really seen products designed with voice in mind—except, perhaps, for Speak & Spell. The rest have added voice input and output as an afterthought. Not so with the next generation of products. The work going on in the research laboratories across the nation is just beginning to make itself felt.

To give you a better feel for the exciting potential of products designed with voice in mind, lets take a look at some of the prototypes built in the labs. If you feel these systems sound like science fiction, they aren't. These systems all exist. Rather than reading science fiction, you are reading tomorrow's news.

ASK THE COMPUTER ABOUT THE WEATHER

The Federal Aviation Administration (FAA) is currently evaluating a system that lets pilots call a computer to find out what the weather will be like along their expected flight path. Mitre Corp. developed the system at its Testbed for Automated Flight Services, in McLean, VA. So far the new system looks promising.

The computerized system directly replaces the existing system. Today, when a pilot wants a weather briefing, he calls the FAA's local Flight Service Station (FSS). The pilot reads his flight plan to a human operator. The operator checks the most recent National Weather Service (NWS) forecast for any areas the pilot will pass through and gives the information to the pilot.

This system works well, but trained flight-service operators cost money. One operator can only handle a few calls each day. Each call requires 100 percent of his attention. And now, there's a better way.

The system under test replaces the human operator. Taking a tip from the order-entry systems, the Mitre system accepts inputs from a touchtone telephone and responds with a voice of its own. The FAA has a special number that pilots call to get the service.

The system uses a large computer constantly updated with forecasts from the NWS. A direct connection between the NWS facilities and the FAA's briefing computer would mean that up to-the-minute forecasts would be obsolete. Computers are fast enough that the system's forcasts could be up-to-the-nanosecond.

But how does the pilot enter his flight plan? That was the design problem that had this voice application held up for a time. Relating a flight path to the weather took some doing. The designers knew that the system had three design goals. It had to be possible for a pilot to call a number and have three things take place:

☐ he had to be able to enter his flight plan;

☐ the system had to be able to relate the weather forecast to the flight plan; and,

☐ the system had to communicate the relevant parts of the forecast to the pilot.

The last item was easy. Voice technology is good enough to provide a suitable voice. The system had to tell it what words to say, however.

The solution came in the form of grid maps. The pilot would plot his flight path on a map marked off in grids and punch in those grid coordinates with the buttons on his telephone. As long as the pilot and the computer both had the same map, all was well. Relating the trip to the forcast proved more difficult.

The NWS provided a method of relating forecasts to map grids. They created a computer database they called the Aviation Route Forecast. Building the database called for taking a close look at the way forecasts were put together. It's fairly easy to say a particular cloud cover will affect certain grid areas, but how do you give some precise measurements to such information? How much cloud cover? At what altitudes?

Examining the forecasts being given to pilots, the NWS found that typical weather information consisted of nonstandardized text messages ranging from five to 40 lines long. Each forecaster had unique descriptions for weather conditions. The factual information contained in the messages had some common factors, however. The messages could be standardized.

A detailed survey established that each forecast, regardless of the variations, could be described in terms of values in 15 categories. They are:

- ☐ Sky condition (cloud cover)
- ☐ Range of cloud bases
- ☐ Remarks pertaining to bases
- ☐ Range of cloud tops
- ☐ Remarks pertaining to cloud tops
- ☐ Surface visibility
- ☐ Weather
- ☐ Freezing level
- ☐ Icing (in clouds above freezing level)
- ☐ Type of icing
- ☐ Turbulence
- ☐ Type of turbulence
- ☐ Height turbulence encountered
- ☐ Weather tops

For each of these, a value represents its intensity, altitude or some other parameter. Each grid is rated in terms of all 15 categories. Thus, the computer knows instantly that in grid 7E the sky condition is one of eight values representing the degree of cloud cover. The system, then, takes the projected flight path information and interrogates its own database, finding out what sort of weather awaits the pilot at each grid along the path.

Figure 7-1 shows you what a typical inquiry might be like. The pilot hits the pushbuttons noted, which indicates he wants to know about the weather at Roanoke, Virginia. The message from the voice-response unit of the system not only describes the current weather in terms of the descriptive categories and values, but also adds general information that could be important. In this case, the remarks refer to snow showers that could alter the forecast.

To give voice to all this vital weather information, the system uses an 800-word vocabulary. Limiting the vocabulary to only these words allowed the system designers to employ a high-quality encoding scheme. The digitization process used in this system takes 25,000 data bits for every second of speech. But the system sounds like a human over the telephone.

Mitre Corporation and the FAA have run several tests in which pilots used the system, and forecasts received from the automatic system were compared with those of the older human-operated system. So far the automated system's forecasts have been good.

Perhaps most important to the success or failure of the system was how the pilots would feel about it. Would they use it? Would they object to dealing with a machine over the telephone? Would they believe the forecasts?

The answer to all these questions seems favorable. The machine handles calls quickly—the pilots appreciated that. The machine can answer more than one telephone line at a time. There's less chance of dialing the briefing number and getting a busy signal.

Further testing will look at the way the systems handles the weather with an eye to improving the system's performance even more. Two possible goals might be to make the spoken forecasts even more understandable by using a variation on the current category-weighting scheme. Alternately, perhaps it's within the power of the existing system to provide pilots with a bit more information about the weather by working on the software.

The current system is a bit large. But then, it's just a testbed. Before such systems are installed for daily use, the designers will have to evaluate the system's real hardware requirements. The testbed facility uses two large minicomputers for real-time analysis and weather-service data processing. These are assisted by two PDP-11/34 minicomputers. Two more PDP-11/34 computers actually handle the incoming calls and voice-response equipment. Much of this equipment won't be necessary when the final requirements of providing a computer with a voice for briefing pilots have been met.

The briefing system's development has contributed much to the understanding of the public's reaction to voice-response equipment, and the techniques for making this equipment available. On an earlier test run, a system using a lower-quality voice was used. It didn't test as well. The information it gave was just as accurate. The voice could be understood well enough. A voice which sounded like a machine's voice, a voice which made the equipment's automation too obvious, wasn't what people wanted. Further studies will determine if these observations are always true or not. In the mean time designers planning systems available to the public have to keep these results in mind.

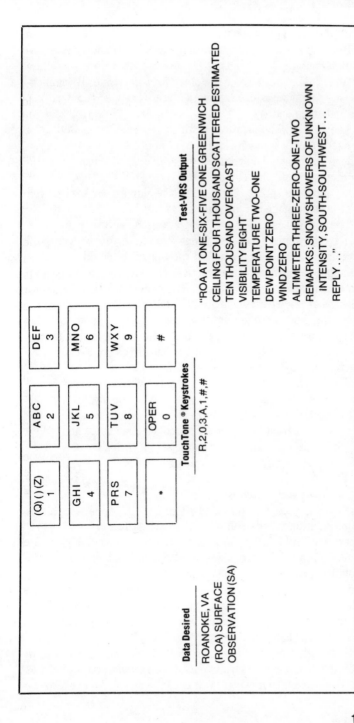

Fig. 7-1. A TouchTone pad lets a pilot input his flight path and receive a weather briefing.

155

A VOICE-CONTROLLED DIALER

Bell Laboratories always rides the vanguard of new communications technology. It comes as no surprise, therefore, that they have been looking at voice technology for some time. Its applications in communications networks are untapped so far, but potentially tremendous.

The first real application in which researchers at Bell Labs have used voice acts much like an electronic telephone directory, a personal directory. You've seen those dialers you can attach to your telephone to dial numbers for you. This one *looks up* the number and *dials* it for you too. But it begins its work when you speak the name of the person you want to call.

The system is called a voice-controlled repertory dialer. A repertory is a place where things are collected or gathered together. In the case of the dialer, the things collected are names and telephone numbers. In a practical system, you would pick up your telephone and speak a name. The dialer looks up the phone number associated with that name and dials it.

If this sounds like just the thing to give someone for Christmas, hold on. It isn't quite to that point yet. Some limitations on the system are still to be overcome before the voice-controlled dialer makes it to the mail-order market.

The prototype system works only within a part of Bell Laboratory's own facilities. There is only one system for all callers. Each caller has to perform two jobs before he can use the dialer: he must train the system to recognize his voice and, while doing that, enter the names and phone numbers that he wants to be able to call. The system doesn't have its own database—yet.

The only thing on the dialer you ever need touch is its mode switch. When the switch is in the training mode (0), the system doesn't try to recognize anything. It accepts the speech inputs as new information to add to its store of speech patterns.

Look at Fig. 7-2. The speech analyzer has two output paths for analyzed data—the recognizer is at the end of one path; the template storage is at the other. When the unit is in its normal-usage mode (1), it draws on the reference patterns stored in the template storage during previous training sessions. The system can't do anything until you have put some names and numbers in this database.

The path from the analyzer to the voice-response system allows the analyzer to let you know it didn't understand what was said. You'll see how it can know it doesn't understand even before

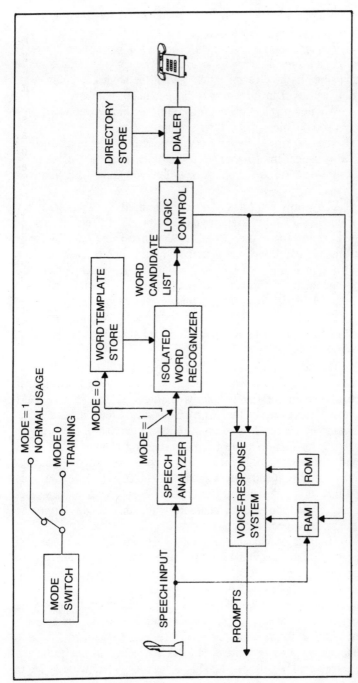

Fig. 7-2. The block diagram for the repertory dialer.

157

the recognizer tries to do its job. The ROM feeding the voice-response system tells it how to say the words in its vocabulary.

You operate the system with your voice. Other than the mode switch, all controls are voice operated. You can instruct the unit to add names to the directory (then give it the names and numbers), delete names in the directory or change a phone number.

Whenever you're using the system the voice-response system helps you do things right. It's a prompting device. It has 13 words and phrases stored in its ROM. You'll hear requests such as "please repeat the number," "at the beep, speak the name to be added" and "please verify." A beep lets you know when it's your turn to talk.

The words you can say are quite limited, but the vocabulary has enough flexibility to allow you to do the job. The commands you need to know to use the system are shown in Table 7-1. The seven commands use telephone terminology in order to pack as much instruction as possible into each command. It's much easier for a system such as this one to pack more operations into each command than it is to add words that must be recognized.

In addition to the seven commands, the system will recognize all ten digits (so that you can enter the telephone numbers) and up to 20 individual names.

The speech analyzer looks for linear-predictive-coding features (LPC) for each word spoken to it. It is these features that actually comprise the templates that get stored in the RAM memory locations called Word Template Store in the block diagram in Fig. 7-2. The analyzer smooths out the words by deriving its feature table from overlapping frames. That is, it divides up each word into 45-millisecond pieces that overlap with the frame in front and in back by 30 milliseconds. Figure 7-3 shows you how this smooths out the data. This approach averages out some of the odd speech characteristics that might otherwise confuse the speech-recognition circuitry.

The analyzer has certain things it looks for in the incoming speech signal. The signal must be large enough for the analyzer to separate the signal from telephone-line noise, for example. The word must be long enough that the system can be sure the incoming signal isn't simply a noise burst, perhaps caused by the telephone equipment. If for any reason the analyzer doubts that the signal is good, it asks for a repeat. The voice-response system asks you to repeat the word or phrase and the procedure of analyzing the speech signal begins afresh. This saves the system from trying to

Table 7-1. The Repertory Dialer's Command List.

Command

OFFHOOK—take the telephone offhook before
            dialing a number
HANGUP—terminate the call
MODIFY (name)—change the telephone number associated
                with (name).
DELETE (name)—delete (name) from directory
ADD—add a new name to the directory
ERROR—disregard the most-recently recognized word
STOP—disregard current command; return to
        command mode

understand a signal that isn't any good. You don't want the template storage to get filled with bad or unusable templates, especially when the solution is so easy. It doesn't take much time at all for a caller to repeat one utterance.

Bell wanted the system to have excellent recognition capabilities. In looking at the techniques various researchers and manufacturers were using successfully, and in reviewing the characteristics of their own application, the team at Bell Labs determined their system would have several qualities:

☐ it would recognize isolated words

☐ it would be speaker dependent

☐ the context of the word being recognized would be important.

The first two points—the system would only recognize isolated words and that speakers would have to train the system to

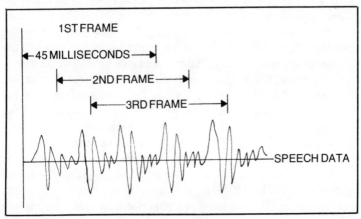

Fig. 7-3. A demonstration of overlapping data frames.

159

accept their voices—reflect the state of the art. These systems have the best track records and the least number of problems to overcome.

The last item—context recognition—not only improves recognition accuracy, it does wonderful things for the speed of that recognition. The system knows that certain words make sense at each point in using the dialer. If you pick up the phone, for example, you won't say a number first. There's no sense in comparing the LPC features of what was received with those of digits, until the digits would mean something. This cuts down on the number of comparisons the system has to make for any given input. The fewer comparisons, the faster the system can decide which template most closely matches the features of the input word. This analysis uses two techniques:

□ **partioned vocabularies**—at each step the word to be recognized falls in a subset of the entire system vocabularly. The subset used depends upon the current context.

□ **semantic constraints**—help determine the proper vocabularly suubset. Entries that don't make any logical sense get automatically disallowed.

A third test ensures the data is good enough to be tested in the first place. This is termed the *rejection threshold*. If the recognition scores are poor, or two stored templates both match the word that was input, the system asks you to repeat the word.

Recognition scores are the means that the system has of choosing what word was spoken. Each word in the proper vocabulary subset gets compared to the input word. The template gets a rating (score) that indicates differences between it and the input word. The template that most closely matches the input word is output as being the word recognized. If the score falls below the rejection threshold, however, no word is chosen. Just as when the analog levels were too low, if the score is too low, there's a danger that the wrong word might be identified. It's better to try again than to identify the wrong word. This is the fail-safe feature of the design. If the system isn't sure what to do, it doesn't do anything except ask again what it was supposed to do. The design follows the adage that "the only stupid question is the one not asked."

As with the pilot-briefing system, the hardware it takes to make the dialer work is a bit unwieldy yet. The prototype at Bell Labs uses a CSP MAP 200 high-speed array processor, attached to a Data General Eclipse computer, to perform the real-time analysis of the incoming speech. Unless you have an empty bedroom to spare, you wouldn't want to consider taking one of these home. It's a lot of system. The jobs it does are reducible, however. Eventually, the computing task might be either simplified or distributed. If it is distributed, perhaps one of our garden-variety microprocessor systems will be able to handle the task. If distributed, the nature of the problem changes a bit.

Distributing the computing tasks implies they are being done in the context of a communication system. Rather than thinking of a dialer that awaits your call, therefore, you should be thinking in terms of a computing system that provides for your communication needs. If it operated under voice control, then it could provide that function for all its elements, including a repertory dialer. Once the voice has been decoded (recognized), the dialing task becomes relatively trivial. You can even buy a single integrated circuit that furnishes nearly all of the components you need to build a dialer. Mostek's MK5170, for example, provides nearly everything you'd need to construct the repertory dialer circuit. Figure 7-4 shows the block diagram for a full-featured repertory dialer. If the system already has a voice-input circuit, you can replace the keyboard shown in the block diagram with the voice-input and voice-response circuitry.

When the researchers were ready to test the voice-actuated dialer system, they used six subjects. Three of these users had never used a voice-recognition system before. Three were men and three were women. These distinctions might be important. Some experts find that experience in using a voice-recognition system results in better recognition scores, indicating there is a way to talk that helps the system understand you. By mixing beginners with old hands, the results would be more accurate.

Voice-recognition systems seem to have normally more difficulty in understanding women than men. Generally, women's voices have a higher pitch than do men's, producing a larger range of frequencies with which the analyzer must contend. Women's voices have more dynamics than men's. The recognition task is, therefore, a bit different for women's voices from what it is for men's.

The six subjects spoke a total of 4692 words to the dialer. There were no recognition errors. This was, to a large extent, because of the feedback system mentioned earlier. When the system wasn't sure of a word, it asked the speaker to repeat the word. The system did this 106 times during the test. That means that less than 2.5 percent of the time the recognizer wasn't sure.

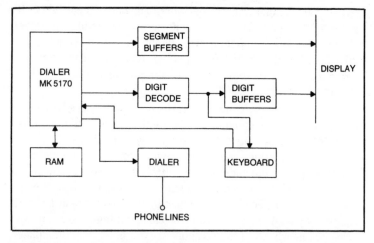

Fig. 7-4. The block diagram of a repertory dialer using integrated circuits.

There's no way to know for certain how many of the words the system asked to be repeated, might have been correct. Remember that the repeat prompt gets issued when recognition scores are low. Low recognition scores don't mean the system can't recognize the word—just that it isn't *sure*.

The recognize and dial operation proved to be fast, too. A complete test took approximately 12 minutes. This means that each cycle—recognize, prompt, response and verify—took between eight and nine seconds, which is pretty quick. You won't find the number in your phone book that quickly.

CHATTY ROBOTS

The telephone dialer makes for a nice tool suited for everyday use, but, except as a demonstration of sophisticated technology, it doesn't exactly tickle our fancy. To find something a bit more esoteric, we look to the world of artificial intelligence.

The entire concept of voice recognition is one sure to delight any artificial intelligence researcher. After all, the decision-making processes involved in selecting a proper word match, especially where you use context to determine a way of narrowing the possibilities, comprises just the type of study that has been going on in artificial intelligence labs for years.

This year marked the introduction of a rolling, talking, listening, example of high technology. Omnivor (Fig. 7-5), a product of a software systems house in Ithaca, NY, called Wolfdata, blends voice recognition, voice synthesis and artificial intelligence (and some solid electronics engineering) into what might be termed the most interactive package to come along.

Omnivor made its debut as a political commentator. Tied into the *New York Times*/Associated Press data bank, it answered any questions on the presidential race, basing its answers on the information it found in the database.

Wolfdata began the Omnivor project on speculation. Engineers at the firm had developed some interesting concepts that needed testing. Omnivor became the test bed. The firm's gamble

Fig. 7-5. Omnivor the Robot uses dynamic updating to ensure that he understands what you say.

has paid off. The self-contained robot's construction, costing approximately $100,000, now falls under a development contract with *Omni* magazine.

The job that *Omni* has in mind for this chatty machine is promotion. Its tasks might include answering telephones to handle science questions that callers might have, giving slide presentations and lecturing. The novelty of having a robot perform these jobs would be sure to attract attention.

To accomplish all this, however, Omnivor must be able to communicate effectively. It must be flexible. Communication comprises a two-way process and implies that the robot not only respond to words, but, in a limited sense at least, understand what is said to it.

The robot's hearing apparatus comprises two directional microphones connected in phase. As the speaker moves, the robot turns its head, keeping the two mikes equally trained on the sound source that it's trying to listen to. This gives the illusion that Omnivor is turning to face the speaker.

Most voice-recognition systems use noise-cancelling microphones, typically worn close to the speaker's mouth, to keep the signal-to-noise ratio low. Obviously, this solution doesn't suit Omnivor's mobile operation. It's also rather difficult to give a telephone caller a special microphone. Wolfdata solved the problem by developing a power-filtering technique that, in essence, removes signal components that could represent noise from the signal it examines. Some of the signal that is thrown away might actually be speech, but it isn't enough to keep Omnivor from understanding and the technique does get rid of the noise.

But eliminating noise doesn't provide word recognition. The input signal must also be analyzed and decoded. Wolfdata considered designing a proprietary recognizer, but opted instead to use the Voice Recognition Module (VRM) from Interstate Electronics. The VRM doesn't provide a complete solution for Omnivor's needs, but its basic recognition of 100 words allowed Wolfdata to supply the rest easily. By combining the VRM's inherent recognition capability with Omnivor's resident intelligence, Wolfdata could write algorithms that recognized words based on their context—their position relative to other words in the sentence. These artificial-intelligence programs also continuously update the VRM's recognition templates, providing dynamic training. Although the VRM is speaker dependent, this dynamic training allows Omnivor to act as if it is speaker independent.

Recognizing words in their context means the robot can "hear" in a manner that approximates the way humans hear and understand.

Omnivor's response to a question can assume two basic forms: verbal and musical. And the two aren't exclusive. The robot could recite poetry to an accompaniment of background music.

Omnivor's voice comes from the same voice synthesizer that Texas Instruments has developed for use in its home computer. The synthesizer provides intelligible speech, but is limited by the size of the vocabulary stored in ROM.

To offset this limitation, Omnivor will eventually incorporate a phoneme synthesizer from Votrax to supplement the current voice-synthesis system. An algorithm will cause the TI unit to output words in its vocabulary and the Votrax unit to supply any additional words to complete a thought.

The music synthesizer helps Omnivor keep pace with human expectations biased by an overdose of *Star Wars*, rather than by any specific need for sound effects. Such a sensational product is forced to live up to the unrealistic billing given robots by writers who aren't engineers. Luckily, however, Wolfdata project leader Carl Frederick considers adding such fine touches among the project's more rewarding tasks.

FLYING SAFELY

Yet another voice system has come into being for the express purpose of aiding pilots. (Which makes one curious as to why so many of the projects that explore the edge of technology are directed at pilots. Are pilots more receptive to new technology than other people?) Small-aircraft pilots flying into airports that don't have control towers often have to guess at important factors, such as wind speed or direction, that affect how they land the plane. That's more, though.

The Automated Pilot Advisory System (APAS) would provide this information over a VHF radio channel without the need for an air controller. The information includes the favored or active runway, position and heading of arriving or departing aircraft, wind information and the altitude of gusts.

A microprocessor provides the voice output. A minicomputer compiles all the information it needs to provide data to pilots. Whenever an aircraft comes within 2.2 nautical miles of the airport, the system begins transmitting voice messages (at 123 MHz) every 20 seconds.

The system illustrated in Fig. 7-6 comprises a prototype. Eventually a totally microprocessor-controlled system might be installed at each of the approximately 500 airports that currently operate without control towers. Eliminating the minicomputer would bring such systems within the budgets of small airports.

AND THE BEAT GOES ON

Because voice technology is still new, it's a bit early to try to guess all of the ways it will ultimately be used. The research effort isn't limited to the prototype systems discussed in this book. As you might imagine, some of the more innovative applications depend on surprising the competition; and then, some companies want to be sure they can make the device before they talk about it.

There are really two lines of speech-research technology. One approach concerns itself with better ways to use existing devices and technologies—improving the performance of current devices. The second arena focuses on new methods of recognizing speech or synthesizing words. These researchers plan the integrated circuits and algorithms that we will use years from now.

In Japan the Ministry of International Trade, in conjunction with Industry's Processing Development Corporation, is developing an intelligent information-processing system. The system will combine a number of processors together in an attempt to solve more complex problems than we have been able to program into computers before. The goal includes having the computer accept spoken problems (word problems) as well as those that are handwritten. The system designers feel it is important that the user be able to draw a geometric shape, for example, and have the computer accept it as part of its input data.

To get such a high performance level, the researchers have suggested that improvements are needed in 12 areas, including: microcircuit design (such as Josephson-junction devices); high-performance processor design (such as Neumann-type data-flow machines); reasoning functions for database machines; ultrahigh-speed large-scale processing; functionally dispersed system architectures; voice-pattern recognition; and computer architecture.

All of these areas actually comprise a single goal—more (better, faster) parallel-processing capability to the point that researchers can emulate the way in which the human mind solves problems. All of the specific considerations are simply breakdowns of this process into functions. It is an attempt to isolate the way we think from the way we hear and see, for example. The voice-

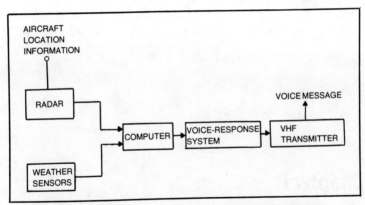

Fig. 7-6. Computer-controlled voice system for automatic ground control.

recognition work would be essential to the overall system concept, but isn't necessary for work to go on in areas relating to the way we process the information once we have it.

So there's a lot of work to be done. And the work that is going on involves a lot of specialties. The results of this research should be such that we find exciting and novel product introductions on a regular basis. And even the speech researchers don't know for certain what those products will be yet.

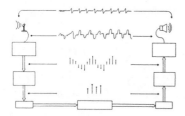

Chapter 8
Adding Ears to Your Microcomputer

The circuits we've discussed so far give you an idea of the nature and application of voice technology. You should have a grasp of the various approaches being used and developed for both speech synthesis and recognition. What still remains is for you to begin working with recognition equipment directly.

Unfortunately, recognition equipment isn't cheap, nor is it particularly well suited to experimentation. Even the lower-cost units are specialized: they have to be in order to provide quality recognition. You can't expect a computer peripheral to cost less than $1000 and provide both speaker-dependent and speaker-independent recognition schemes just so you can try them out.

This is changing, however, Interstate Electronics Corp. has introduced three new chip sets that might signal a price break-through. The 2A chip set gives you 95 percent recognition-accuracy ratios for 24 phrases. Interstate's 2B chip set lets you custom-select the phrases. Most importantly, perhaps, the chip set designated 3 furnishes speaker-independent recognition of four to eight words with an 85 percent accuracy ratio. This last chip set also provides voice response.

But don't hold your breath waiting for someone to announce a new product using these chips. In the first place, the chips aren't available in quantities of less than 100,000. Secondly, it will take some development time before other manufacturers feel comfort-able using chips supplied by just one manufacturer.

Another avenue you might pursue in locating a voice-input circuit parallels the discussion of voice synthesis. If you've noticed that the 2920 (Intel) could be used as easily for speech input as for output, then you're one jump ahead of most engineers. In fact, the chip is a preview of chips to come, chips that will directly attack voice-recognition problems. The only reason for not using one of these chips for experimentation is that it gives you inventor's tunnel vision. While they minimize the number of parts it takes to build a given circuit, they also dictate the approaches available to you in solving the recognition problem.

Suppose, for example, that you don't think any sort of filtering improves recognition. It might be that the information contained in the speech wave is encoded in a manner not obvious from traditional electronic viewpoints. The 2920 chip provides versatile signal-processing capability, but within the boundaries of electronic conventions.

You must begin to think of such chips (at least for experimentation) as nothing more than specialized tools—not solutions. And the experimenter can't afford to carry a large inventory of specialized tools. What you'll need, therefore, is an understanding of how to use discrete components to test out various theories, theories usually discussed as circuits; elements in a block diagram.

The voice-recognition laboratory we will build becomes a framework for constructing specific equipment. This might sound like a reversal of the conventional approach to putting together a laboratory, but it makes more sense than buying one of every speech device available. If you can build the specific circuits, or models of those circuits, then you can develop an understanding of the theory and practice of recognition that will allow you to evaluate any commercial recognizer.

THE SPEECH LABORATORY

You will have to have some basic equipment for working with the circuits you wish to test out. Some kind of computer—any kind of computer—makes configuring and reconfiguring the circuits much easier. You then have the option of doing specific parts of the task either in hardware or software. We will evaluate how to make that decision later on, but the point that is important for now is that the computer provides flexibility.

Our speech laboratory will be based on Synertek System Corporation's (Box 552, Santa Clara, CA 95052) SYM-1. The SYM-1 uses a 6502 microprocessor and suits the needs of this book for one important reason—it is simple. It also costs only $380 when you buy a complete package from Sybex (2344 Sixth St. Berkeley,

CA 94710), and that includes a course that gets you started using the computer.

You won't need to get very deep into computer hardware to build the circuits in this chapter. We will take advantage of a special chip that comes on the SYM-1 to save a lot of work and complication. This chip, the 6522 versatile interface adapter (VIA) is another reason for choosing the 6502 microprocessor as the basis for the experimentation. This device provides, among other features, a PIO just like that used for the Z80 voice-output module shown in Chapter Six. You'll see how that will make life quite easy as we go.

A basic speech-input experiment will have to perform three functions:

☐ **listening**—converting ascoustic signals to electrical impulses

☐ **conversion**—making the analog waveforms digital

☐ **understanding**—matching the received patterns to something previously stored.

No matter how simple or complex the design, unless you use an analog processor you'll have to perform all three to accomplish speech or speaker recognition. With our laboratory defined, we can begin some experiments to see how this might be accomplished.

A SIMPLE RECOGNITION PERIPHERAL

In this chapter we will tackle one rather cumbersome way of recognizing speech and design a simple peripheral that will accomplish the task well enough to convince ourselves that the task can be accomplished. First, we must look at the overall function of the recognizer. As shown in Fig. 8-1, we must input speech, convert it to digital, then identify the digital patterns. This, logically enough, corresponds directly to the three tasks a recognizer must accomplish (which you saw earlier). This figure is known, for that reason, as a functional block diagram. You'll notice that nothing in the diagram indicates what kind of hardware or software will be used. Nothing is noted about the technology. Rather, this abstract will serve only to guide our thinking.

Although it is an abstract, not a design, the functional block takes us through some important design decisions. For it is this document, the skeleton of a design, that we will begin to flesh out. We will insert enough detail into the block's sweeping generalizations to give the design a direction and then some specific guidelines. The block breeds the schematic.

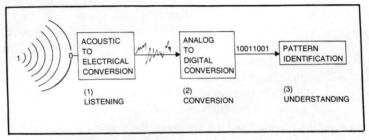

Fig. 8-1. The recognition process.

Before you can even begin to think about what parts to solder where, it's important to take a close look at the job that must be done, the limitations and potential of the available equipment and the nature of the input signal.

The acoustic-to-electrical conversion task is one that can be handled any number of ways, depending on the nature of the input signal. When you hear, your ear does that job nicely. In the inner ear, small hairs, called cochlea, convert the vibrations of the inner ear's bones into neural impulses. The brain handles the word identification and any other processing (such as context analysis). That, then, is the detailed block diagram for the human word-recognition system.

By analogy, you can begin to see how you might just do a one-for-one redesign to add ears to your computer. The processor takes the role of the brain. The analog-to-digital circuits (we will look at these in detail later) act in lieu of the cochlea and a microphone fills in for the ears. Thus, we have the block diagram laid out in terms of both the task (by analogy with nature) and the equipment available to us. Figure 8-2 shows how far this takes the design process. You still could not build a working speech-recognition system from the drawings, but we have taken the development process a giant step further. At least the functional blocks represent more specific circuits.

To keep the design and operation simple—and transferable to other microcomputer systems—the circuit will operate as a standalone peripheral. The microcomputer won't furnish any timing or synchronization functions. The recognizer must accept speech and take its samples without any assistance from the processor. You'll be able to use this circuit, therefore, along with a processor that has other tasks to perform.

The overall system specification calls for a peripheral that will:

171

☐ recognize when a word is present at its input

☐ divide the analog input into two energy bands—one accommodating the low-frequency signal, and one handling everything in the high-frequency range

☐ sample the signal in each energy band

☐ convert the samples to digital values

☐ pass the values to the computer

Each digital sample will be 8 bits long. Each 8-bit sample has the possibility of being one of 256 discrete values, providing a dynamic range of 48.2 dB for each sample.

Because the peripheral doesn't depend on the processor for its timing information, the control logic must take over the job. Although this complicates the peripheral's design, it does take quite a load off the processor; and, in fact, makes it possible for you to use this same design with almost any microcomputer.

It seems appropriate, therefore, that we stay in line with contemporary computer jargon. Our circuit, as shown by the block diagram, has begun to take shape; therefore it needs a name. More exactly it needs an acronym. The unit accepts words. Let us call it a word-input module: WIM. It is the first of its kind; thus, WIM-1.

To understand the WIM-1's circuits, we will start at the input and look at what the circuits do at each point in the signal processing. Remember this is a demonstration circuit, however. We are presenting an easy-to-build-and-use approach, not the best technique for word recognition. Once you understand the circuit, we will discuss the software you'll need to begin recognizing words and the changes you might make to extend the recognition capabilities of the WIM-1.

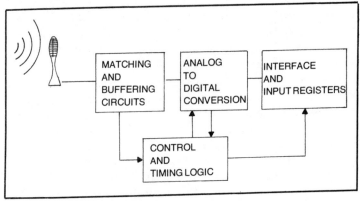

Fig. 8-2. A recognition peripheral.

THE INPUT CIRCUIT

The input circuitry, the ears in our electronic hearing system, has several functions. The circuits must provide:

- ☐ input buffering
- ☐ isolation
- ☐ gain
- ☐ level translation

The first two items, input buffering and isolation, are two sides of one coin. You want the acoustic signal to enter the circuits (so it can be heard), but you don't want the recognizer to radiate a signal of its own. That is buffering. You don't want anything the recognizer is doing to alter the input signal. That is isolation.

The gain function makes sure the signal will be large enough to be identified. It also ensures the signal won't be too large for the next stage to handle. The gain might be negative in such a case.

Level translation also means impedance matching. Our input transducer (a device that transforms a physical stimulus into an electrical charge) will, like the rest of the design, be the simplest possible. The best bet is a common garden-variety microphone. The input circuit must accept the microphone output and provide an output that suits the rest of the design.

You can use almost any available microphone for our recognizer. The type that comes with cassette tape recorders suits the job admirably. Using an expensive electret microphone might improve the system's performance some, but not to any effective degree. If you have a good quality microphone, go ahead and use it. But don't go out and buy one for this recognizer.

For our cheap, high-impedance microphone, the circuit shown in Fig. 8-3 meets most of the requirements of the input circuit. Although nothing more than a unity gain follower (the output voltage equals the input voltage), the circuit buffers the input, provides isolation and will match the next stage perfectly. If you use a single-supply op amp, such as the LM158, you'll need to add two resistors, as shown in Fig. 8-4. By adjusting R2 you can control the gain from unity (when the resistance equals 100K) to a factor of 10.

Once you have isolated the WIM-1 from the outside world and made sure you have enough signal with which to work, it is time to do some signal processing. The first stage of the circuit shown in Fig. 8-5 eliminates low-frequency noise. Everything below 100 Hz gets attenuated. Next, the analog input divides up by spectrum.

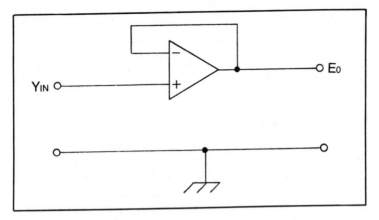

Fig. 8-3. A unity gain buffer.

The low-frequency signals go in one direction; the high-frequency signals (above 1 kHz) go in another. This lets you analyze the signal in terms of two parameters—the energy contained in each band at a certain time in an utterance acts as a fingerprint (although crude) for the word.

The circuit shown in Fig. 8-6 adds additional bits of information about the incoming word—it tells the logic when a word is present.

The envelope detector is adjustable. It takes its input from the output of the noise-suppression circuit in Fig. 8-5 (point C). This helps eliminate triggering on noise—a condition that can take place whenever the ambient noise is quite high relative to the signal.

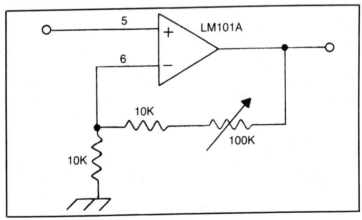

Fig. 8-4. A buffer with adjustable gain.

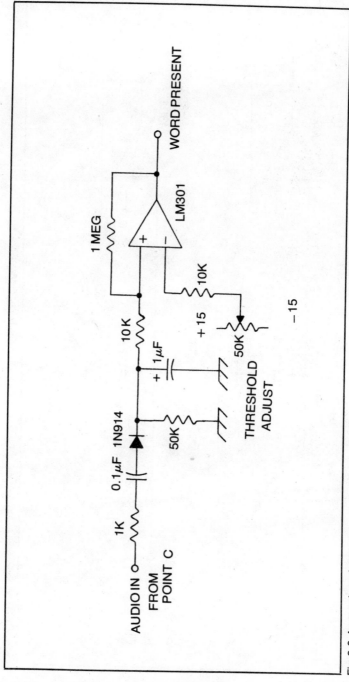

Fig. 8-6. An envelope detector.

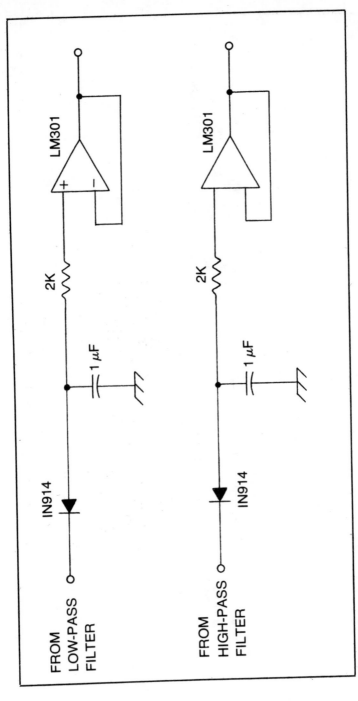

Fig. 8-7. Stabilizing the analog values.

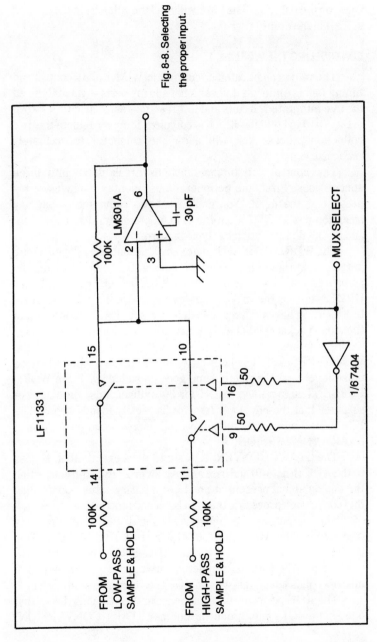

Fig. 8-8. Selecting the proper input.

EOC (end of conversion) signal goes to the logic. This signal coordinates much of the activities of the WIM-1.

When the ADC converts a value, it outputs it as an 8-bit binary value on the data bus. The 6522 will read the value from the bus and store it in the proper register.

CONTROLLING THE WORLD

The most complicated circuit in the WIM-1 is its control and timing logic. Although it doesn't have many parts—you only need the five integrated circuits and few resistors and capacitors shown in Fig. 8-10 to build it—its job is complex. It must regulate the data collection process that will allow the computer to accurately recognize words.

The control and timing functions break down into three specific jobs. First, the peripheral must identify when a word is present at the input. You don't want the computer to pay any attention to the WIM-1 until it has completed its data collection, and it can't do that until it has heard a word.

The WORD PRESENT logic signal, produced by the envelope detector, initiates the chain of events that will provide the computer with its sample values. WORD PRESENT will stay HIGH as long as the analog input level is above the reference level to which you have the envelope detector set. The first one-shot in the dual package labeled IC1 provides a 20-millisecond delay before anything else happens. This will help make sure that the WORD PRESENT signal was false, such as might happen when the noise level near the microphone goes up suddenly. If the WORD PRESENT signal stays HIGH for 20 milliseconds, the one-shot assumes that the envelope detector has really found a word. The IC's second one-shot then outputs a 2-microsecond pulse termed START CONVERSION.

The START CONVERSION signal does exactly that. It goes to the ADC (Fig. 8-9) and causes the converter to begin converting the analog signal present at pin 12 to a binary value. Controlling this conversion process is the logic's second function.

The output of the high-pass sample and hold circuit is connected to the ADC when the MUX SELECT line is LOW. This is the signal therefore, that the ADC begins converting immediately. When it has completed this task (approximately 100 microseconds later), it issues an EOC (end of conversion) signal.

The EOC performs two functions: first, it toggles the second one-shot in IC1 again, producing another START CONVERSION.

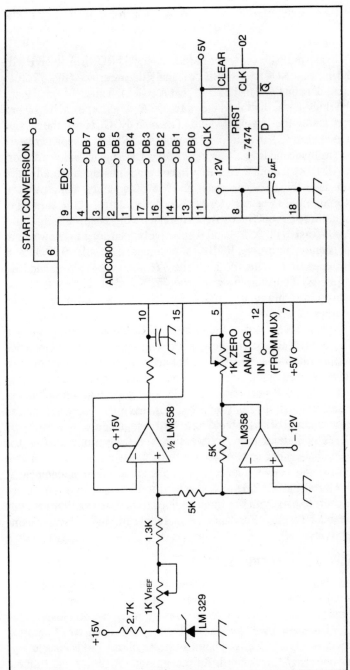

Fig. 8-9. The conversion circuitry.

181

It also toggles the JK flip flop in IC3 which , in turn, toggles the MUX SELECT line HIGH, connecting the low-pass signals to the converter.

A 1-millisecond timer in IC1 causes STROBE A to go HIGH during this EOC. STROBE A signals the interface (the 6522) to input data on the data bus into port A (ORA). Thus, the 6522 loads the high-pass digital value into ORA while the ADC begins converting the low-pass value. The next EOC causes the second one-shot in IC1 to reset, and produces STROBE B approximately one millisecond later. This inputs the ADC's binary value into port B (ORB) of the 6522. You now have two 8-bit values stored in the interface chip. The high-pass and low-pass values will always be stored in the same register. This orderly control of the passing of values into the 6522 constitutes the logic's third task.

To use STROBE A and B effectively, you need to know where to connect them. STROBE A becomes CA1 and STROBE B becomes CB1 on the 6522. On the SY6522, CA1 is pin 40 and CB1 is pin 18. You must program the 6522 to shift data in when the appropriate pin goes HIGH, but this is a relatively simple operation.

Now take a look at the more detailed block diagram shown in Fig. 8-11. You can see how this circuit qualifies as a standalone peripheral. It does everything that needs to be done to get the two values stored in the computer. Thus, it takes care of the listening and conversion portions of the block diagram that served as the initial product specification. You now have the schematic for an experimental basis for building a word recognizer.

The listening and conversion are fairly quick. After the 20-millisecond delay to get you into the word and to eliminate performing conversion of aspirations rather than phonemes, it should take about 2.5 milliseconds to store both samples. You can, of course, play with the timing values to find delays that give you the best results. For such a simple circuit, the values become arbitrary.

MAKING SENSE OF NUMBERS

The task of providing understanding falls to the software. You'll need to develop a program that suits your own needs, but some basic principles and techniques will apply nonetheless.

Take, for example, the fact that you'll need two operation modes—one that lets you build a pattern library (your vocabulary) and one that accepts words for recognition. These are the training

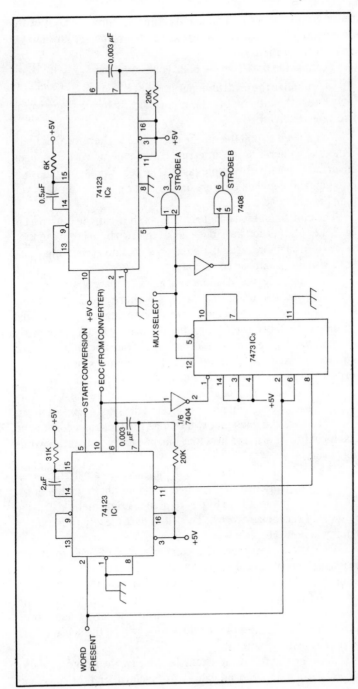

Fig. 8-10. The timing and control logic.

183

and operating modes. Training is simple. Simply input word patterns in a known order using exactly the same speaker as you will use in operation.

To input the data from the 6522 you'll need to:

☐ initialize the 6522 for input

☐ test the interrupt register periodically to see if any words have been received.

You'll need to poll the device periodically, therefore, or find a method of generating an interrupt whenever a word has been converted (a relatively simple task). The technique you choose is up to you and depends entirely on the other system software you might have or need.

The polling method handles input, as shown in the flowchart in Fig. 8-12. All this software does is put the two bytes representing the word in memory. You'll also need a routine comparing these bytes with the prestored vocabulary.

Unfortunately, you'll seldom get an exact match between your input data and the prestored patterns. There are far too many variables at work in producing as well as listening to, speech. What you should do, therefore, is limit the vocabulary to a few distinctly different words. Test a few words. Input your vocabulary words into memory and look at the two bytes they are stored as. Use words with large differences in their two bytes from other words.

Your evaluations should always begin with the most significant bits of each word. Temporarily discard the least-significant four bits. These are the ones that will change the most and convey the least meaning. It is in the first four bits of each byte that the words should vary.

The analysis algorithm should compare the most-significant bits first too. Only use the last four bits for subtler distinctions. The flowchart presented in Fig. 8-13 gives a crude method of using the data to recognize words. This flowchart merely illustrates a technique; however, it is worth a closer look.

What takes place here is a comparison of the values of two vocabulary words and the input pattern. In each case, first the routine finds out which value is largest. You want the result to be positive. The routine then subtracts the smaller of the two—the input value or the reference pattern—from the larger and stores the results. The smaller of the two results will be the score that is closest to the input pattern.

Consider the following example. In a two-word vocabulary, one word has the high-band value of 4 (decimal) and the low-band

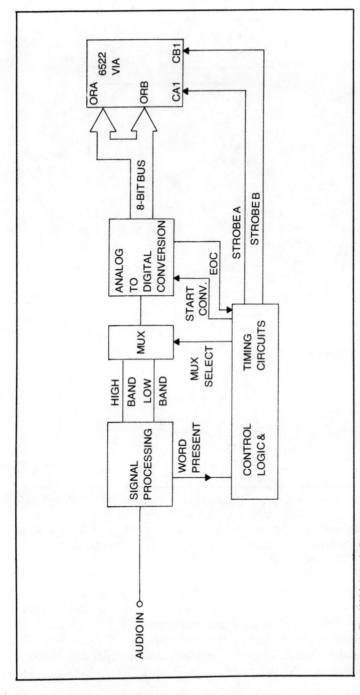

Fig. 8-11. The WIM-1 block diagram.

185

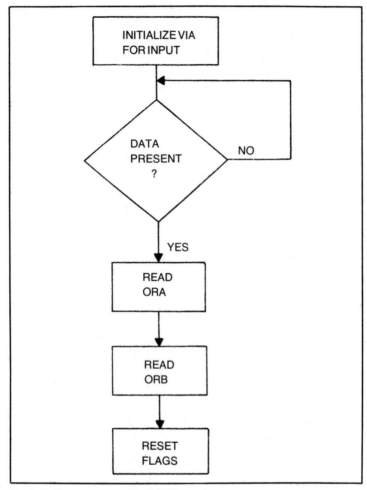

Fig. 8-12. The computer polls the 6522.

value of 8. The second word has values of 120 and 110, respectively. The input word is represented by 80 and 50.

The input byte of 80 is compared to the 4; the operation of 80−4=76. The 80 is then compared to the 120, yielding 40. The input value of 50 is compared to the 8, producing 42; compared to the 110 it produces 60. Add the two passes together and the input data differs from the first reference pattern by 118; compared to the second reference pattern the input data scores 100. The crude algorithm would, of course, conclude that the input data matched the second reference pattern best. What you'll have to experiment

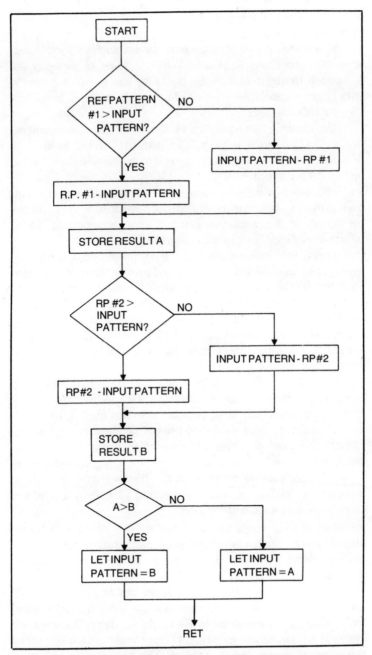

Fig. 8-13. You determine which pattern has the values closest to that of the input data.

with is to see if a difference of 18 (out of 100) is significant. You might need to retry.

This close call points up the need for developing an additional level of recognition software. You will have to develop an arbitration routine that sets the limits for close calls, especially with larger vocabularies where several words might all be within 20 points of each other.

The example also points up the shortcomings of the circuit as designed. Two bytes is very little data with which to make a decision. You might, therefore, choose to complicate the circuit a bit to get more information.

The envelope detector measures the length of the word, or at least provides a timing mark suitable for measuring it. By counting the length of the word you can add another important bit of information. Going back to our example, if you knew, in addition to the scores, that reference pattern #1 represented a word that averages 65 milliseconds in length and pattern #2 represented a word that was 35 milliseconds, you would be able to compare those to the input word's length as another scoring element. If the input word was 40 milliseconds long it would support the close call and maintain that #2 was the correct match. A 70-millisecond measurement would be further proof that you should try that word again, however.

It won't take much circuitry to add this data to your WIM-1. In fact, all you need is another 6522 in the 6502's address space. And there is another modification you can make that might prove even more significant. What if you had several samples throughout the word, rather than one 2-byte data sample? Theoretically you would be able to throw out the data at the extremes and average the remaining samples to obtain patterns that will vary less from utterance to utterance. Your recognition scheme will produce more reliable results, better scores.

The penalty you'll pay for improving accuracy will be in slightly more complex circuitry, more storage space required for each input-word data sample and more complex code needed to analyze the data properly.

This brings you to the same dilemma faced by researchers in commercial applications. You must evaluate these tradeoffs. How much memory can you afford to use for date and program storage? How much time can you spend identifying the correct word? This is the accuracy versus speed problem. The better you make your recognition algorithm—that is, the more data points you look at—the longer it takes. You run a risk of developing an algorithm with ludicrous time constraints. Imagine a system that was 100% accurate but could only accept a word every five minutes.

IMPROVING RECOGNITION

If you glance at something or someone and there is a familiar feeling, you will usually look again. This is the process of taking a better look. But why is the second look better than the first? The second look can take advantage of information you acquired during the first look.

Suppose you see a person walking down the street, and she looks familiar. During the next look you won't waste time gathering and sorting through a lot of peripheral information. You know that you are looking at a female person and that there is a high degree of probability it is someone you already know. Thus, you can concentrate your efforts on gathering clues that will add specific information.

Now let's apply this same strategy to voice recognition. This time, suppose you modify the timing circuits to take *two* samples during each word—two in the high-energy band and two in the low-energy band, that is. If the first sample (we will consider each 2-byte operation as one sample) is the same as our previous example, you can use the information to narrow down recognition possibilities.

The best illustration of the practicality of this process is to re-examine our example and add some new vocabulary words. Previously we proposed a two-word vocabulary. In decimal notation (for our convenience) our input word scored 80 (high band) and 50 (low band). The first reference pattern scored 118 (difference from the input data); the second pattern scored 100.

Table 8-1 plots those scores along with the scores for two new vocabulary scores. A quick look tells you that, although the scores for reference pattern #1 and #2 are far apart, the input word could

Table 8-1. Example Value-Comparison Data.

	Input Data	Reference Patterns #1 Difference		#2 Difference		#3 Diff.		#4 Diff.	
HIGH	80	4	76	120	40	10	70	200	120
LOW	50	8	42	110	60	120	70	200	150
TOTAL			118		100		140		270

be representing either one. Obviously noise or some other factor has corrupted the input data somewhat.

The data for words #3 and #4 are not much of a problem. Even our crude algorithm could easily weed out these word candidates. The problem still lies in determining which of the two words is actually the correct match.

One method of collecting data is to match two data points. Suppose for our vocabulary words and for the input words you had configured the system to take and store two samples. Table 8-2 provides a possible readout of those data points. There might be no resemblance between a given word's first data points and its second. The data will be highly dependent on the exact time the data is taken.

One method of taking advantage of two samples is to average the difference data. This would provide scores of:

☐ 80 +118=198   198/2=99
☐ 200+100=300   300/2=150
☐ 90+140=230   230/2=115
☐ 150+270=420   420/2=210

While this method gives, with reasonable certainty, a clear match betwen the input word and reference pattern #1, it requires several math operations. This might not be the best method of performing recognition. Furthermore, it involves performing all operations on every possible word candidate. Word pattern #4, for example, clearly wasn't even in the running after the first match. Its 270 difference score indicated that there was not a likelihood of it being even close to the right word.

One approach that would speed recognition time while increasing accuracy is to eliminate these dark horse words as soon as possible. Suppose, after the first pass, the computer calculates the difference between the two best scores (18) doubles it (36), and then throws out all words that exceed the total of the best match's score plus the doubled difference. In our example, the computer

Table 8-2. A Second Pass Provides Additional Data.

	INPUT WORD	#1		#2		#3		#4	
HIGH	10	90	80	110	100	50	40	10	80
LOW	60	60	0	160	100	10	50	130	70
TOTAL			80		200		90		150

would eliminate both word patterns 3 and 4 after the first pass. Both exceed 136.

The elimination process means that the decision is down to selecting the best of two. Our second match indicates that pattern #1 is much closer than pattern #2. No other calculations are necessary.

The fact that the first pass was so ambiguous indicates there is yet another technique needed to protect the long-term accuracy of the system. Although, through using two passes, the recognition was made, the first pass indicated that there is a problem, either in the reference patterns or in the data collected.

Although it is quite possible, and even probable, that the variance from the reference patterns came from external noise, it could also arise because the speaker's voice has changed over time. To ensure that this doesn't cause problems, you need a method of updating the reference patterns periodically.

Certainly you can retrain the WIM-1 periodically. But this approach involves unnecessary training time. The patterns don't need updating daily; but some days they will definitely need them. The simplest way to check on the need for retraining is to output the matching scores.

You could print the word that was recognized on the cathode-ray tube screen of the computer. In parentheses, next to the word, you could print out the matched word's score, a dash, then the score of the next best word.

If you match all words on each pass (no elimination process), then in the example the printout might look like:

WORD #1 (99—115)

Rather than WORD #1, the recognized word, such as POWER, would be printed. The 99 is WORD #1's matching score; the 115 is the score of WORD #3.

If you used the elimination process, you would see:

WORD #1 (99—150)

Because you eliminated WORD #3 in the first round, the score looks better. Still, 99 is quite a ways from perfect. You'll have to experiment with your recognizer to determine what is a good score for your specific application and vocabulary. Remember that the more diverse you vocabulary is—the greater difference in the words' scores—the easier the recognition is and the wider matching tolerances you can accept. When selecting your vocabulary, you might find it beneficial to put the WIM-1 in its train mode and test various words. Look at the reference patterns. If two words have quite similar values, the computer won't be able to distinguish between them.

Once you have become familiar with your WIM-1's operation, you might want to add another technique to improve long-term accuracy. You can use virtually every input word to retrain the reference patterns. Once you have identified a word, by averaging the current values with the previous values, you can update the patterns *dynamically*.

Going back to our trusty example, we can take a look at how dynamic updating works. When the program prints

WORD #1 (99—150)

on the screen, you already know whether or not WORD #1 is indeed the input word. You might make the operator acknowledge the word (for training and learning purposes—otherwise this defeats the point of voice input) or simply assume that the computer will pick the right word frequently enough to make dynamic updating useful. The flowchart shown in Fig. 8-14 illustrates the updating process. The 80 averages with the 4; the 50 with the 8; the 10 with the 90; the 60 with the 60. The sample number and high/low status must be maintained. Reference pattern #1 will now have the values shown in Fig. 8-15. Note that if you were to input the same word, and get the same input data, the difference score for pattern #1 would be 48.5 rather than 99.

Theoretically, some sort of averaging scheme would allow the recognizer to track any changes in the speaker's voice, whether due to time or environment. You probably find that the simple averaging scheme just outlined is a bit too radical, however. If you've got enough memory space in your computer, the best bet is to try some sort of moving average. A moving average is an approach that uses several data points, not just two. You could use a 4-point average, for example. This would match any incoming word to the average of the four previous samples.

To start with, you would provide four training scores (say each word four times). The computer would then store all four scores, plus the average of the four. Using just the averages, the computer would then recognize a word. The very first sample stored would then be erased and replaced by the current value, which would be averaged in with the other three to produce a new average for matching. Thus, at any point in time, the input word is matched with reference patterns which are the result of averaging the last four samples. This eliminates radical changes due to short-run changes in the background noise or a speaker's voice while tracking real changes in the way a person is actually saying any given word.

Again, however, the tradeoff for using a sophisticated algorithm to dynamically update the patterns is in the time it takes to make the calculations and the memory required to store the data.

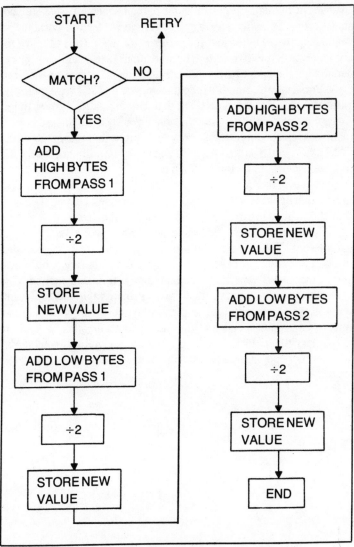

Fig. 8-14. Dynamic updating helps the recognizer track reality.

	1st Sample	2nd Sample
HIGH	42	50
LOW	29	60

Table 8-3. The Updated Reference Pattern Provides Better Scores When Compared to Current Data.

The four-sample moving average (moving, because it follows changes in the data) requires eight bytes for sample storage and another two bytes for storing the average. A 4-word vocabulary would require 40 bytes just for pattern storages! You still have to accommodate the two bytes for the input word and the space needed for the updating program. Plus, this only handles the first pass. For accurate, reliable recognition, you'll want to use multiple passes. A word provides patterns that vary dramatically over time. To capture any of the flavor of the word, you should plan on using as many passes as you have memory for. But at this rate, a 10-word vocabulary, with four passes (say one every 10 milliseconds for 40 milliseconds) would require 400 bytes!

These techniques won't provide accurate recognition. You must experiment to see which ones provide useful data. Then and only then can you write routines that will use the data.

Remember when we discussed using word length as a parameter? With this information you might be able to speed the word-elimination process. Yet, if all the vocabulary words are about the same length, you can't apply this information. By carefully selecting words with different sample values and different lengths, you can simplify the pattern-matching process and use fewer data points. Where the application dictates a certain vocabulary that doesn't lend itself to easy recognition, you'll have to apply more sophisticated software to the task.

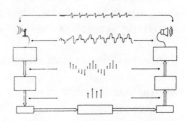

Glossary

acoustics—the study of all sounds.

allophone—any of the variant forms of a phoneme after it has been conditioned by its position in a word or by other phonemes.

analog—an information system that allows the signal to vary continuously.

ASCII—American Standard Code for Information Interchange. An information code comprising seven data bits and one parity bit for error checking.

artificial intelligence—a scientific research area where scientists attempt to make machines behave and respond as humans do.

aural—referring to the sense of hearing.

bandwidth—the difference between the limiting frequencies of a continuous-frequency band. Also, the transfer speed of digital information.

binary digit—a unit in the binary notation system. It can be ZERO or ONE.

binary logic—digital-logic elements which operate in two distinct states.

binary number—a number comprising binary digits.

bit—a binary digit.

compiler—a computer program that translates high-level program statements into codes the computer understands.

computer—a device that can accept information, apply prescribed processes to the data and output the results.

continuant—a speech sound that can be sustained or continued over a period of time such as "s," "m" or "r."

continuous speech—words and phrases not necessarily separated by perceptible pauses. Normal human speech.

data rate—the speed of information flow, usually described in bits per second (bps).

digital—an information system that uses discrete voltage levels to represent data.

discrete speech—utterances (words or phrases) separated by perceptible (approximately 100-millisecond) pauses.

discrete-word recognizer—a computer-control device operating under the control of a human voice. Allows data entry of isolated words and numbers into formatted data fields.

dumb terminal—a computer-control and data-entry device with no local intelligence.

execution—the processing of a computer instruction.

formant—a frequency range containing more energy than surrounding ranges; a frequency burst amplified by the vocal tract.

frication—an audible airflow disturbance caused by molecules under great pressure being forced into molecules under less pressure.

global—an underlying or base process that applies to all data, as opposed to some specific construct.

high-level language—a computer programming structure that allows you to express a number of machine-level operations with one programming statement.

iterative—repetitious; the cyclic application of some process.

lateral—a speech sound caused by air escaping from the mouth laterally.

morpheme—any word part that conveys meaning.

morphology—the study of word structures.

nasality—the qualities added to the speech signal by its passage through the nasal cavity.

orthography—a spelling system.

overtones—multiples of the fundamental frequency.

phonemes—the basic speech sounds.

phonemics—the study of phonemes within a particular language.

phonetics—the study of speech sounds, their production, combination and representation.

phonology—the study of the natural processes and rules which manifest themselves in a natural language.

resonant—a voiced speech sound that uses one or more of the vocal tract's resonant cavities. Includes sounds such as "r," "m" or "n."

utterance—a speech phrase.

waveform— the shape of an analog signal.

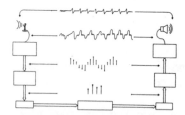

Appendix A

Equipment Manufacturers

The following list includes companies involved in research into speech technology and companies manufacturing speech equipment.

American Hospital Supply Company
H. C. Electronics Division
250 Camino Alto
Mill Valley, CA 94941

Auricle Inc.
20823 Stevens Creek Blvd.
Cupertino, CA 95014
(408) 257-9830

Calma Company
5155 Old Ironsides Drive
Santa Clara, CA 95050
(408)727-0121

Centigram Corporation
155A Moffet Park Drive
Suite 108
Sunnyvale, CA 94086
(408)734-3222

Cognitronics Corporation
25 Crescent St.
Stamford, CT 06906
(203) 327-5307

Computalker Consultants
Box 1951
Santa Monica, CA 90406
(213) 392-5230

Consumer Microcircuits
114 E. Simmons St.
Galesburg, IL 61401
(309) 342-8196

Costronics Electronics
13 Field Heath Ave.
Hillingdon, Middlesex
England

East Coast Micro Products
1307 Beltram Court
Odenton, MD

E.G. & G.
45 Willia- St.
Wellesley, MA 02181
(617) 237-5100

E-Systems Inc.
Box 6030
Dallas, TX 75222
(214) 742-9471

General Health Corporation
1046 Potomac St. NW
Washington, D.C. 20007
(202) 965-4881

General Instruments
600 W. John St.
Hicksville, NY 11802
(516) 732-3107

Harris Semiconductor
Box 883
Melbourne, FL 32901
(305) 724-7407

Heuristics Inc.
1285 Hammerwood Ave.
Sunnyvale, CA 94086
(408) 734-8532

Hitachi America Ltd.
2700 River Rd.
Des Plaines, IL 60018
(312) 298-0840

Intel Corporation
3065 Bowers Ave.
Santa Clara, CA 95051

Interstate Electronics Corporation
Box 3117
Anaheim, CA 92803
(714) 635-7210

ITT Semiconductors
Box 749
Lawrence, MA 01841
(617) 688-1881

Kurzweil Computer Products Inc.
33 Cambridge Parkway
Cambridge, MA 02142
(617) 864-4700

Logicon Inc.
21535 Hawthorne Blvd.
Suite 440
Torrance, CA 90503
(213) 325-6060

Maryland Computer Services Inc.
502 Rock Spring Ave.
Belair, MD 21014
(301) 838-8888

Master Specialties Company
1640 Monrovia Ave.
Costa Mesa, CA 92627
(714) 642-2427

Mimic Electronics Company
Box 921
Acton, MA 01720
(617) 263-5837

Mitsubishi Electrical Corporation
2-12 Marunouchi Chiyoda-ku
Tokyo, Japan

Mostek Corporation
Network Applications
Box 169 MS 535
Carrollton, TX 75006

Motorola Semiconductor Products Inc.
Box 20912
Phoenix, AZ 85036
(602) 244-6900

Mountain Hardware
300 Harvey Blvd.
Santa Cruz, CA 95060
(408) 429-8000

National Semiconductor Corporation
2900 Semiconductor Drive
Santa Clara, CA 95051
(408) 737-5864

NEC America Inc.
532 Broadhollow Rd.
Melville, NY 11746
(516) 752-9700

Omnicron Electronics Corporation
1 Mechanics Street
Putnam, CT 06260
(203) 928-0377

Panasonic Company
One Panasonic Way
Secaucus, NJ 07094
(201) 348-7275

Percom Data Company Inc.
211 N. Kirby
Garland, TX 75042

Quintrex Inc.
9185 Bond Ave.
Overland Park, KS 66214
(913) 888-3353

Scott Instruments
815 N. Elm
Denton, TX 76201
(817) 387-1054

Speek Up Software
3491 River Way
San Antonio, TX 78230

Sperry Univac
Univac Park
Box 3525
St. Paul, MN 55165

Sun Electronics Corporation
38, Mizuho, Kochino
Konan City, Aichi, Japan

Technology Service Corporation
2950 31st St.
Santa Monica, CA 90405
(213) 450-9753

Telesensory Systems
3408 Hillview Ave.
Palo Alto, CA 94304
(415) 493-2626

Texas Instruments Inc.
8600 Commerce Park Drive
Suite 100
Houston, TX 77036

Threshold Technology
1829 Underwood Blvd.
Delran, NJ 08075
(609) 461-9200

Toshiba America Ltd.
Consumer Electronics Division
280 Park Ave.
New York, NY 10017

Transcom
580 Spring St.
Windsor Locks, CT 06096
(203) 623-2481

Tri Formation Systems
3132 SE Jay Street
Stewart, FL 33494

Verbex Corporation (formerly Dialog Systems Inc.)
Two Oak Park
Bedford, MA 01730
(617) 275-5160

Voice-tek
Box 388
Goleta, CA 93017
(805) 687-8608

Votrax
500 Stephenson Highway
Troy, MI 48084
(313) 588-2050

Appendix B
Additional Reading Material

The following are most of the books available on the subject of voice input and output. All of them in some way contributed to making this book better.

Artificial Intelligence, edited by A. Bundy. 1978, Edinburgh University Press, 22 George Square, Edinburgh, England. This is not specifically a voice book, but it will help you understand some of the approaches taken by artificial intelligence research.

Automatic Speech and Speaker Recognition, edited by N. Rex Dixon and Thomas B. Martin. 1979, IEEE Press. John Wiley & Sons Inc., 605 Third Ave, New York, NY 10016. Includes papers by leading researchers.

Speech Analysis, edited by Ronald Schafer and John D. Markel. 1979, IEEE Press. John Wiley & Sons Inc. More papers, including Homer Dudley's work.

Speech Synthesis, by Cecil Coker, Peter Denes, Elliot Pinson all of Bell Telephone Laboratories. 1963, Comspace Corporation, Farmingdale, L. I., NY 11735. This includes a simple vowel-synthesizer kit and a short book on speech basics for synthesis. An excellent starting point for the nonengineer.

Trends in Speech Recognition, by Wayne Lea. 1980, Prentice-Hall, Englewood Cliffs, NJ 07632. A top-flight collection of speech recognition papers.

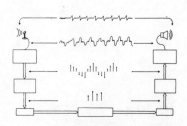

Appendix C

ARPABET Symbols

These symbols allow you to efficiently represent phonemes in a computer.

PHONEME	ASCII CHARACTERS	EXAMPLE	PHONEME	ASCII CHARACTERS	EXAMPLE
i	IY	beat	p	P	pet
I	IH	bit	t	T	ten
e	EY	bait	k	K	kit
ε	EH	bet	b	B	bet
χ	AE	bat	d	D	debt
α	AA	bob	g	G	get
Λ	AH	but	h	HH	hat
ɔ	AO	bought	f	F	fat
o	OW	boat	θ	TH	thing
U	UH	book	s	S	sat
u	UW	boot	ʃ	SH	shut
ə	AX	about	v	V	vat
ɪ	IX	roses	δ	DH	that
ξ	ER	bird	z	Z	zoo
αU	AW	down	ž or 3	ZH	azure
αI or αy	AY	buy	V c	CH	church
αI or αy	OY	boy	ζ	JH	judge
y	Y	you	M	WH	which
w	W	wit	syl 1, ḷ	EL	battle
r	R	rent	syl m, m̩	EM	bottom
l	L	let	syl n, n̩	EN	button
m	M	met	flapped t	DX	batter
n	N	net	glottal stop	Q	
η	NX	sing	silence	-	

205

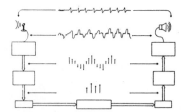

Index

A

Acoustic remote
controlled system | 105
Adaptive differential
pulse code modulation | 66
ADC | 46
ADPCM | 66
Advisory system, automated pilot | 165
Allophone | 34
Allphones | 84
Amplifier, single-chip operational | 149
Analog-to-digital converter | 46
APAS | 165
APU | 47
ARCS | 105
ARPABET phonetic spelling | 74
Articulation | 38
ASR | 93
Audio playback unit | 47
Auto correlation, partial | 53
Automated pilot advisory system | 165
Automatic speech recognition | 93

C

CDS | 82
CERL | 79
Chatty chips, other | 146
Chatty robots | 162
Chips, chatty | 146
Circuit, input | 173
Coding, linear-predictive | 52
Compander | 116
Computer-based
education research laboratory | 79
Continuant | 79

Continuous-speech systems | 94
Continuously variable
slope delta modulator | 120
Controller, phoneme access | 141
Controlling the world | 180
Conversion | 170
Conversion | 180
Converter, analog-to-digital | 46
Customer development system | 82
CVSD | 120

D

D/A | 48
Dedicated suppliers | 20
Delta modulation | 117
Dependent, speaker | 94
Dialer, voice-controlled | 156
Digital things | 176
Digital-to-analog | 48
Drawing crazy patterns | 92

E

Education research
laboratory, computer-based | 79
Electronic engineering | 13
Emulator | 82
Encoder-decoder, voice | 122
EOC | 180
Equipment manufacturers | 66
Establishing the rules | 76
Extraneous recognition | 112

F

FAA | 151
False recognition | 112

Federal Aviation Administration 151
FIFO 47
First-in, first-out 47
Flight Service Station 151
Flying safely 165
Fricative 79
Friendly software 13
FSS 151

H

Handicapped, helping the 22
Human engineering 13

I

Improving recognition 189
Independent, speaker 94
Input circuit 173
Integration circuit, large-scale 148
Intermorphemic phenomena 80
Invisible articulation 38
Isolated-word recognizers 93
Isolation, taking words out of 105

L

Laboratory, speech 169
Large-scale integration circuit 148
Lateral 79
Learning to speak speech 28
Listening 170
Listening to anyone 108
Linear-predictive coding 52
Linear-predictive-coding 158
Low-cost recognition 98
LPC chips,
    unrestricted speech from 84
LPC 52
LPC 65
LPC 158
LSI 148

M

Making sense of numbers 182
Mix the strategies 77
Model speaker 40
Modulation, delta 117
Modulation, continuously
    variable slope delta 120
Morpheme 34
Morphological features 78

N

Nasal 79
National Weather Service 151
NEC 106
Nippon electric company 106
No recognition 112

Numbers, making sense of 182
NWS 151

O

OEM 66
Op amp 149
Optacon Print Reading System 24
Original equipment manufacturers 66
Orthographic characters 76

P

Parameter encoding 65
Parameters, speech 39
PARCOR 53
Partial autocorrelation 53
Peripheral, recognition 170
Physics of speech 36
Picking a recognizer 110
Programming
    produces phonemes 72
Phonematics 34
Phoneme access controller 141
Phoneme interaction 76
Phonemes 34
    programming 72
Prosodic features 39

R

Read-only memory 47
Recognition 90
    extraneous 112
    false 112
    improving 189
    low-cost 98
    no 112
    peripheral, simple 170
    voice 91
Recognizer, picking 110
Recognizers, isolated-word 93
Recognizers you can buy 94
Rejection threshold 160
Resonant 79
Robots, chatty 162
ROM 47
Rules, establishing 76

S

Segmented-speech systems 93
Simple approach 127
Single-chip operational amplifier 149
Software, friendly 13
Sounds of speech 34
Sounds, putting together 39
Speaker dependent 94
    independent 94
    model 40

Speaking differently 52
Specialized systems 104
Speech chips 47
Speech laboratory 169
    PAC 141
    parameters 39
    physics 36
    sounds 34
    unrestricted 84
    without restriction 58
Speech systems, continuous 94
Speech systems, segmented 93
Speeding up things 79
Store sounds, not words 70
Suppliers, dedicated 20
Synthesis 44
Synthesizers by themselves 60
Synthesizer, match
    to the application 69
Synthesizer, putting to work 132
Systems, acoustic
    remote controlled 105
Systems, specialized 104

T

Taking words out of isolation 105
Talk buffer 138
Talking data bases 19
Talk to machines 26
Telecommunications 114
TLKBFR 138

U

Understanding 170
Utterances 93

V

VDES 96
VET 101
Visible articulation 38
Vocoder 122
Voders 44
VOICE 96
    control 15
    controlled dialer 156
    data entry system 96
    encoder-decoder 122
    entry 91
    entry terminal 101
    oriented core executive 96
    recognition 91
    recognition module 30
    recognition module 94
    recognition module 164
    response 91
Voices pre-recorded 44
VRM 30
VRM 94
VRM 164

W

Word structures, uncovering 78
World, controlling the 180